LOVE: The Missing Ingredient

Brenda J. Stephens

ISBN 979-8-88832-781-4 (paperback)
ISBN 979-8-88832-782-1 (digital)

Christian Faith Publishing
832 Park Avenue
Meadville, PA 16335
www.christianfaithpublishing.com

All biblical citations were taken from the King James Version of the Holy Bible unless otherwise indicated.

Printed in the United States of America

Introduction

This book is for all men. The love of God is for all men, and this book is about the love of a Creator who wants all men to know how much He loves His creation. It is not the story of my life. It is the story of my cry to God concerning the lack of love in the church and the answer that was revealed to me. This answer is not just for me but for all who hunger to love and be loved. The events that I speak of are merely personal or eyewitness of situations that caused me to cry to God seeking answers and are applicable to most people who either seek or shun the church experience and what God has to say about it.

In 1988, I asked God a question that started me on a path of learning and experience with Him that I have not begun to see the total fulfillment of, but I am engrossed in the midst of it. The question was, "Why have you never said that to me?" You see, my sister was showing me the word that she had received from God in Revelations 3:7–13 where Jesus speaks to the Church of Philadelphia, the love church. I thought that was a mighty word to receive from God. I wondered why He had never said that to me. Am I not in the "love church"? Am I not walking in love toward people, showing love to all people?

Two of my sisters and I had been experiencing adverse situations in the new church that God had lead us to. Each of us dealt with the situations that we encountered in different ways. My older sister chose to leave the church and went off seeking a more suitable fellowship. I chose not to leave the church but to leave off fellowshipping with people that are hurtful and deceiving. My younger sister continued to attend the church and fellowship with the people that were so hypocritical and phony. I remember being so annoyed with my younger sister for being so gullible and ignoring the wrong that was being done to her while she continued to fellowship with those who would talk about and make fun of her then smile in her face.

Often we think because we are putting up with people, tolerating people, that we are walking in love and showing the love of God to all people, but that is not the case, and so it was with me. I asked God a question and did not get an answer for over a year. During this time, I began to read scriptures and buy books on love to see what God had to say to me about my love walk. I listened to Christian radio and television programs and made every effort to be where the word of God was being preached so that perhaps God would give me an answer and perhaps that answer for me would be the same as His word to my sister. It is amazing how God will use another to make one jealous for His love and attention. Yes, I was jealous. I wanted to know that God loved me and saw me in the same light as my sister. Well, I found that I had a lot to learn and a lot of growing to do. Yes, God loves me. God loves all His creation. The question is, do I love Him and all His creation the way that He loves me? I can, because the Holy Spirit pours the love of God into the hearts of all of us who receive His Son as Lord and Savior of our lives (Rom. 5:5.) However, do I? That is the question.

At the beginning of the same year, God had spoken to me in a dream, a long night vision. He showed me what He had done, what He was doing, and what was yet to come. More than half of what God showed me in that dream on the second Sunday of March in 1988 has come to pass. However, there is still much that is to come, and patiently I wait for it. Immediately after the dream, God spoke to me audibly and told me to go to a new church. I started hearing the voice of the Holy Spirit when I was a little girl attending a Baptist church and had come to know His voice well. I knew that God was speaking to me and fully understood what He was telling me to do. However, I was not so willing to obey. Well, we know that Jesus told the disciples, "If you love me, keep my commandments." In other words, if you love me, obey me. So here was an excellent example of my love walk because when God told me to go to this new church, I immediately asked why and told God that I was not going over there. It's really funny how we think that we are there, we are so holy, so righteous, and have our Christian walk so together, and yet we can't even obey a simple command such as go to that church.

It took me fourteen months to obey God. I was holding on to where I was tooth and nail. After all, it was hard enough becoming adjusted to this church. I began to argue and plead with God, asking Him, "Why that church?" The pastor of the new church was once a minister of the church that I was currently attending. This minister had participated in spreading lying gossip about me all over the church. For three years I was an outcast in the church, during which the first year and a half I was out of fellowship. It took the painful miscarriage and loss of twin daughters to get me back on track with God and back into church. Even after returning to church, I continued to endure the upturned noses and snotty attitudes of the holier-than-thous. I spent another year and a half trying to prove to the people in the church that I was not the person that I was accused of being. After three years of being treated like I was the most wicked woman alive, I decided that was enough. I decided that I could not leave this church and go to another because this is where God sent me. Nevertheless, I will spare myself the misery of being bothered with these people by only attending once a month. I determined that I would fill myself up on television and radio ministry and Christian books. I had my whole lineup planned. Saturdays from noon to 5:00 p.m. I would listen favorite pastors and teachers like Bishop William L. Bonner, Bishop Ralph E. Green, and Bishop Joseph Weathers. But a word from God and an act of God turned me around, and I spent another two and a half years in sweet fellowship with God and His people.

Now, after all that I have been through trying to be a part of this church and You would send me over there where that minister is now the pastor. Noooo, I am not going over there. Lord, you know that I spent the first three years being lied on, falsely accused, mistreated, and gossiped about over here, and that minister helped cause all of that. Now You are telling me to go over to the church where he is the pastor. God, You know how You had to deal with people about how they were toward me and the wrong that they did to me. You know how You had to deliver me and lift me up. Now I am a happy usher, singing in the choir; I am the president of the church newsletter printing staff. God, You know that if I don't make sure this newsletter is put together right, then it will not be done. You know how people are, God; they say that they are going to do something, but when you need them to help, you can't find them. God, You know what happened when I asked Sister So-and-so to help me. You know the mess that she brought back to me at the last minute, and I did not have time to fix it. God, You know I have to get this newsletter out, so if I don't stay here for any other reason, I need to stay here for this.

Excuses, excuses—we all have them, and I had mine. We never stop to think about what Jesus suffered for us. We never stop to think about what Jesus gave up coming to the earth and living and walking as a man, suffering with our sins and dying on the cross of Calvary for us. What a shame.

After things started falling apart for me, I started to wake up. I thank God for ministers like Elder Fields. He always seemed to know just where I was spiritually and emotionally. He always seemed to know how to pray for me and what to do for me, even if it hurt. So in December of 1988, Elder Fields made an adjustment and replaced me as the president of the newsletter printing staff with another member of the church. He obviously knew that I was holding on to this responsibility and using it as an excuse to not obey God and go to this new church. I was hurt, but I knew it had to happen. I had to obey God, and he had to replace me. Yet it took another five months for me to get up the nerve to leave the place where I had become so comfortable even though it was not so comfortable anymore. But I prayed and asked God to go before me and prepare my way. Finally, I left to go to the next place God had for me.

Therefore, in May of 1989, I arrived to the new church deliberately late for service hoping that I would go unnoticed by the members. Wouldn't you know that service was late starting that morning? Not only was I noticed, but the response that I received from the pastor was totally surprising to me and alerting to the rest of the small congregation. It was so surprising that I was not sure how to respond to my new church environment. Now I was really about to begin learning about my love walk and the missing ingredient that would bring the peace, joy, prosperity, and fellowship with God that I so desperately desired. I got to this new church and found out that the pastor was a graduate of Rhema Bible Training Center founded by Kenneth E. Hagin. I was really excited about that because I had read so many of Brother Hagin's books, which helped me to grow spiritually and know when I am hearing from God and how to follow Him. I learned that Kenneth E. Hagin held a camp meeting in July of every year, and this year's camp meeting was coming up soon. I wondered if this was the place that God had shown me four years earlier in May of 1985. I went all the way to San Jose, California, looking for this place. Could this camp meeting be what God showed me? I made special effort to get there, and I can tell you it was one of the greatest experiences of my life.

I experienced a lot during the first three months of my membership in this new church and immediately after this camp meeting. Things were said and done that almost broke me and drove me to my knees seeking God for answers. For the better part of my life, I spent years crying to God about the cruelty and sinfulness of church people. I was born attending a Baptist church where my grandmother was the head deaconess. Grandma had a serious attitude about church attendance, and on Sundays, her house was emptied. She knew she could not make the adult men go to church, but she would not allow them to lie around in her house when they could be in church. Everyone had to get out of her house on Sunday. All the children had to go to church, and my mother had to go to take care of us children.

I often wondered what good it did. My father was still a hell-raiser. He beat my mother brutally, neglected his children, and ran around with his White lawyer girlfriend that got him off any legal charges he incurred. I emphasized White only because in the '50s and '60s, mixed marriages and relationships were illegal in Virginia, and Black women lawyers were few and far in between. In fact, most of the Black women in my neighbor were undereducated like my mother, who only completed the fifth grade. As a young child under my grandmother's influence, I went to Sunday school. I learned Psalms 23, the Lord's Prayer, and the Ten Commandments. They teach these main Bible verses in the Baptist church. Church itself was fine as long as Grandma was alive. After all, no one messed with Mrs. Essie's grandchildren. Then Grandma died, and it seemed like all hell broke loose. There ceased to be any peace in church anywhere. My aunt, my father's sister, hated my mother because my mother was fair complexioned and had so many children, and my aunt was dark complexioned and had no children. If I sat in the main floor of the sanctuary and fell asleep during service, my aunt found reasons to call and pick fights with my mother. If I sat in the balcony, the older kids would pick at me so that I would yell at them to leave me alone. Then, of course, my aunt would call my mother and pick fights with her over that. Unfortunately, when my mother was able to get away from my father, she met another devil worse than my father, and her lifestyle changed for the worst. Then, instead of going to church, she sent her children to church, the older ones looking after the younger. We became a laughing stock. We were considered "a bunch of bastard children of a lazy woman who would rather lie up with that man than get up off of her behind and bring those children to church." Well, that is what they said, and my own auntie was the leader of the pack. Never mind their own sins, their drinking, whoremongering, adultery, and lasciviousness. Far too many times we church folk are too busy pointing fingers at someone else to take a good look at ourselves. Love would have loved my mother and her children and drawn us back to church rather than mistreat us and push us away. This became such a frustration that at the tender age of eleven, I dropped out of church completely.

I became a single unwed mother at the age of twenty. At twenty-one, I inherited my late brother's Bible, and not knowing where to start, I decided I would start reading in the New Testament because I figured anything new must replace the old and that is where the stories of Jesus began. I read all of Matthew and understood most of what I read. Then I got into Mark and could not understand why the same stories were repeated, so I skipped the repeats. The same was true with Luke, and John was initially confusing but seemed to clear up as I got through the first chapter. I was fortunate enough to get through most of the New Testament with enough understanding as to what kind of person I should be. However, I did not understand words like *fornication, licentiousness, idolatry,* and *dissension* and just decided I would look them up when I got to a dictionary. The problem with that is either I never got to a dictionary or I never remembered to look up these words. So for years I never knew what they meant and continued to wallow in sin in these areas.

At age twenty-four, I decided while I was not in church, I could at least read the Bible to my daughter. Initially, this seemed easy. After all, I had gone to Sunday school and learned a little something. My relationship with God had not changed. I still believed in God, and loved Jesus, just not church people. But reading the Bible to my daughter was not as easy as it seemed. For her I decided to start at the beginning with the Old Testament.

I got through Genesis fine, and Exodus was okay until I got to the building of the Tabernacle and the word *breadth* and *cubit.* What is a breadth or a cubit? They did not teach us these words in school, and I did not have a dictionary to look up the meaning of these words. So okay, skip that, and skip that until I finally skipped right into Leviticus. Oh my goodness, what in the world is a burnt offering, and what kind of animal split the hoof and chew the cud? What is a hoof and a cud? Lord, have mercy, I did not have a dictionary handy, and I needed some help with this stuff. Right off the bat, I was in trouble in this chapter. So okay, I'll put off reading to my daughter until I learn something for myself. I managed to get to chapter 11 of Leviticus. However, when I got to the words *hoof, cloven-footed,* and *chewing the cud,* that was it. I am a stone-cold city girl. At the age of twenty-one had barely seen a cow and certainly not close up, so without a dictionary I was lost. Well, that was it. We are out of here, daughter. Time to go back to church. Years later when I read the story in the book of Acts about the Ethiopian eunuch again, I knew just how he felt. How can I understand unless someone guides me?

The very next Sunday I was up bright and early to catch the bus and get to Sunday school by 9:30 a.m. Unfortunately, this proved to be fruitless. Sunday school for me was awful. The associate pastor was teaching the class, and he was a wolf in sheep's clothing. There were only four of us: the associate pastor, his wife, another man around my age, and me. The associate pastor drooled across the table at me and decided to change the teaching topic from the ETTA Sunday school booklet that we were supposed to be reading to his own topic, which was David and all his wives and children. He iterated the only thing wrong with David and all his wives and all his children was not keeping control of them all. Well, this was my first and last day back to Sunday school for the next decade or so. When I picked my daughter up from her Sunday school class, I could tell that her experience was no better. So again, I was out of Sunday school and, before long, back out of church. The cruelty and criticism was now coupled with lust and left no room for a single young woman like me to learn the word of God.

This was when I seriously began to pray to God about church people. As a child, I simply lamented. But as an adult, I somehow knew I needed to be in church, and I really wanted to learn how to live right, but where? How? All I knew is what I had learned and seen growing up. My mother's father was an illiterate man who beat his wife and neglected his family. My mother's mother died when my mother was five years old, and she never received another mother or older woman to teach her how to be a woman. My grandfather gave my mother to my father when she was sixteen years old with two children by two other men. My father was a rapist who raped my mother to have sex with her and beat her to keep her. My brothers learned what they saw my father doing to my mother, and one of them began practicing the same with one of my older sisters and me. I was molested from the time I was two or three years old until I was around eight or nine years old. I lost my virginity to my own brother. While attempting to persuade me to go along with the molestation, it was engrained in me that girls have sex with boys and women have sex with men. The whole purpose of a girl or a woman was to have sex with a boy or a man. If this was right, why were we beaten when we were caught? Even though this somehow did not seem right to me, it is what I learned. Unfortunately, I was never taught any boundaries. If you are going to have a boyfriend, then you are supposed to have sex with him. If you want someone to take care of you and provide for you, then you have to have a boyfriend. So you had one at home and one on the side, even in the church.

However, as a single mother raising my children without their fathers beside me to help, I just knew in my heart that there was something wrong with this way of living, and I wanted to learn how to live right. That became the cry of my heart, and I know that there are many others in the world just like me. What church shall I go to where the people are not cruel, lustful, holier-than-thou, phony, perverted hypocrites? So of course it was hard leading me into my first Pentecostal church, and I was there five and a half years of which the first three were so difficult that it almost broke me. Now I have obeyed God and come to this new charismatic church, and I find myself crying to God again. If God so loved the world that He gave His only Son, and if Jesus so loved the Father that He obeyed even to death on the cross, and if the love of God is poured out into our hearts by the Holy Spirit, why am I not feeling it?

Finally, on a Saturday afternoon in August of 1989, I was alone in the living room of the apartment where I lived with my niece, crying out to God and continuing the prayer meeting I had just left with my new church family when the Spirit of the Lord began to speak to me. The content of this book is what God spoke to me, and I will now endeavor to share with you what God spoke to me that day. My earnest prayer is that it will be as profound and enlightening for you as it was for me.

1

Eight Things

I had just left a prayer meeting with my new church family. The pastor had arrived with a certain church member who was upset about something that he had said to her. What did he say to her to hurt her like that? As I pondered on this, a second thought came to me, and I turned and looked at the pastor of this small church and realized that he was watching my observation of this member with a look that said, "Now, how about that." I was floored, so to speak. How could a pastor of the church act like that? What had he said to her, and why did he think that it was okay to make a person hurt like that without taking heed to his own ways? That member's prayer request was for God to help her to love people in spite of their faults, lifting her head just long enough to glance at me while stating her request. In the midst of her stating her request, she had to stop and confess that she knew that she also had faults. Yet she needed help to love others in spite of their faults. We all have faults and shortcomings, and while we are seeking help to love others, we need to seek help in examining our own hearts. That is where the real cleansing begins.

Now the prayer meeting was over, and I left there feeling like we had not prayed at all. I had no peace in my spirit, and I felt like we had just gone through the motions but had not gotten through to God, and I just needed to continue and pursue Him for myself, for the pastor and this church member. So I gathered myself, my Bible, and my writing pad and cried out to God for an answer. I desperately needed to know where is the love, how do we get to it, and how do we walk in it. As I was praying and crying to God, the Holy Spirit began to speak, and this is what He said:

> *Charity suffereth long, and is kind; charity envieth not; charity vaunteth not itself, is not puffed up, doth not behave itself unseemly, seeketh not her won, is not easily provoked, thinketh no evil; rejoiceth not in iniquity, but rejoiceth in the truth; beareth all things, believeth all things, hopeth all things, endureth all things. Charity never faileth. (1 Cor. 13:4–8)*

There are eight things that love does and eight things that love does not do.

Things love do:

1. Love suffers long.
2. Love is kind.
3. Love rejoices in truth.
4. Love bears all things.
5. Love believes all things.
6. Love hopes all things.
7. Love endures all things.
8. Love never fails—it continues.

Things love does not do:

1. Love does not envy.
2. Love does not vaunt itself.
3. Love is not puffed up.
4. Love does not behave unseemly.
5. Love does not seek her own—is not selfish.
6. Love is not easily provoked.
7. Love does not think evil.
8. Love does not rejoice in iniquity.

To fully understand what Paul is saying and the significance of the eight things, you must have some understanding of biblical numerology and the Jewish number system. Neither the Hebrew nor Greek language have characters for numbers. There are only letters, and the letters have numeric value which is called the Gematria. The manner in which the letter is used determines whether it represent a number or a letter. This being the case, every word also has a numeric value. For example, calculating the Gematria of the name Jesus derives the number 888. In Greek, the name Jesus is *Iasous* and has the following numeric value: Observe, $i = 10$, $a = 8$, $s = 200$, $o = 70$, $u = 400$, $s = 200$. Adding these numbers together, you get 888.

One is the number of unity. In one, there is no room for difference, and it refers to that which is sovereignty. It represents the Father as indicated in Deuteronomy 6:4, "Hear, O Israel: The Lord our God, the Lord is one," thus emphasizing there is one true and living God, and we should worship Him and Him alone. In Ephesians, the Apostle Paul makes a very similar statement. Declaring God's unity and oneness, he states, "There is one Lord, one faith, one baptism, one God and Father of us all." There is no difference in one, and it represents sovereignty in that it is independent of other numbers. Yet it is the source of all numbers thus representing the sovereignty of God who is independent of all in existence yet the source of all existence.

Two is the number of division, or difference. While the division or difference maybe good or bad, it usually speaks of opposition, enmity, and oppression. It is the first number that can be used to divide another number. Wherever there are two in a situation, there must be agreement; otherwise, there is opposition. In Amos 3:3, the prophet asks the question, "Can two walk together except they agree?" Hence, where two exist, there must be agreement or opposition.

Three is the number of the trinity: the Father, the Son, and the Holy Spirit. It is the number that makes for substance. One or two lines make a plane, but a third line is required to enclose space. Adding a third line makes a cube and provides a means for substance. Therefore, three stands for that which is solid, real, substantial, complete, and entire. Its symbol is the cube, which is the least complicated form of solid matter.

Four is the number of creation and refers to the Earth, sun, moon, stars, and the constellation in the heavens. It is the number of material completion because it was on the fourth day that God finished all material creation, as we know it. Included in material creation is groupings of four. There are four elements—earth, air, fire, and water. The earth has four physical locations—north, south, east, and west. There are four segments to every day—morning, noon, evening, and night. There are four season—spring, summer, fall, and winter. Even the moon has four visibilities—full moon, first quarter, half moon, second quarter. There many other emphases of four as with all the numbers in scripture; however, it is too much to be included in this writing.

Five is the number of grace. It represents the favor of God in the earth. It represents the redemption of man from sin. When God called Abraham and made a covenant with him, there were five sacrifices used in the covenant—a heifer, a goat, a ram, a dove, and a pigeon (Gen. 15:8–15).

Six is the number of man. Man was created on the sixth day. It can be viewed as grace (5) with God (1) or creation, which is man's world (4) with division (2) or (1) short of spiritual perfection (7). God created man to be perfect. But when man sinned in the garden of Eden, he became separated from God, fell short of spiritual completion, and needed God's grace to be reunited with Him; hence, 4+2, 7-1, 5+1 all equal 6.

Seven is the number of perfection and represents that which is complete. The word *seven* is *shevah*. It is derived from *savah* which means "to be full" or "satisfied, have enough of." On the seventh day, God's work was finished and completed, and He rested from all His work and blessed and sanctified the seventh day, thus representing spiritual completion.

Eight in Hebrew is *Sh'moneh* derived from *Shah'meyn* meaning "to make fat," "cover with fat," "to super-abound." As a participle, it means "one who abounds in strength." As a noun, it means "super-abundant fertility." Numerically it is the superabundant number.

Since seven represents completion and rest, and eight is an extension beyond seven, then eight is the first of a new series and represents the number of new beginnings. This number is most interesting to me because I am the eighth-born child to my mother. My parents never married until she thought she was pregnant with me. I am different from all my siblings, and the one closest to being like me is the one born immediately after me. She and I are the only two born in marriage, and she (number nine) is the last of my father's children and marked the end of that relationship. I will address the number nine more toward the end of this book. For further information on the symbolic representation of number in the Bible, see *Number in Scripture* by E. W. Bullinger or *Biblical Numerology* by John J. Davis. However, for the purpose of this study, I will concentrate on the number eight.

Eight is the number of fruitfulness, productiveness, and usefulness. It also represents value, worth, and utility. As I meditate on this, I understand why the Holy Spirit revealed these eight things to me about love. Love is a creative force. God is love, and through His love, He created the heavens and the earth and all that is in it. It is only as we walk in the agape love of God that we are fruitful, productive, and useful. It is on that which we love that we place value and worth. That is why it is imperative that we learn to operate in the love of God so that our values are properly placed and the kingdom of God is edified.

The number for the name Jesus is 888. It is said to be the perfect expression of perfection. Jesus was perfect in love. He is our perfect example of walking in love. He is God's representation of love in the earth, and as we study His life in line with Paul's Epistle to the Corinthians, we will come to understand why Jesus said the "works I do ye shall do also."

Notice when Paul was teaching this word to the Corinthian Church, he started with the first two things that love does: (1) love suffers long, and (2) love is kind. Then there is a sudden shift, and Apostle Paul switches over and gives all eight things that love does not do. You see, we must suffer long with the infirmities of others and continue to be kind. To be kind, we must mortify the deeds of our body and put off all of our ungodly ways, which consist of all of the things that love does not do *before* we can get to the rest of the things that love does do: (1) love does not envy, (2) love does not exalt itself, (3) love is not puffed up or conceited, (4) love does not behave unseemly, (5) love is not selfish (seeks not her own), (6) love is not easily provoked, (7) love thinks no evil, and (8) love does not rejoice in iniquity.

Then the Holy Spirit, through Paul, switches back and completes the things love does: (3) love rejoices in truth, (4) love bears all things, (5) believes all things, (6) hopes all things, (7) endures all things, and (8) love never fails, or in other words, love prevails.

In this passage, I believe the Holy Spirit speaking through Paul was trying to get a point across to the body of Christ, and that is simply, we must love as He loves. God suffers long with His creation and has been more than kind to all of us, especially those of us who profess to know and love Him but cannot seem to put away our sin long enough to have a decent relationship with him. Notice that we must get past the first two things that love does to get to all eight of the things that love does not do. You see, first we must learn how to suffer and endure hardship and still be nice. Then we must learn how to not be all those things that we don't like to have to deal with in others before we can get to all the rest of the things that love does. Eight is the number of new beginnings, perfection, and fatness. When we began to love like Jesus loves, then our love will become perfect, and the creative force of God will become explosively effective in our lives. Then we will move into the fourth dimension of the creative power of God.

2

Love Suffers Long

Charity suffereth long.

—1 Corinthians 13:4

The Holy Spirit speaking through Paul starts off with love suffers long because that is exact what God has done for man since Adam first sinned in the garden of Eden. God loves His creation and first demonstrates His love through His patience and long-suffering toward our sin.

The Greek word translated suffer in this text is *Makrothumeo* and actually means to be long-spirited, objectively forbearing and subjectively patient, bear long, or patiently endure. God demonstrates this to us every day by putting up with us in our self-righteous mess. He demonstrated this same love to Adam and Eve in the garden of Eden. God could have just wiped Adam and Eve out and started all over again. But instead He showed them love and made the first blood sacrifice to cover their sin. Although there were consequences to pay for committing high treason and selling out to Satan, God had already made the way to redeem man from sin. He pronounced the means for our salvation in Genesis 3:15, and it showed up four thousand years later in the person of Jesus Christ.

In the process of those four thousand years before the birth of Christ, God continues to show His love for His creation by bearing long and patiently enduring man's apostasy of abandoning Him and turning to other gods, worshipping them. God made the first blood sacrifice to cover Adam's sin. It is evident that Adam learned from God and taught his children about the requirement for a blood sacrifice for sin. We see this in Genesis 4:1–10 in the story of Cain and Abel. They both brought sacrifices, but Cain chose to bring the sacrifice of his own choosing rather than that which God required. When he saw that his sacrifice was not acceptable to God because it was not what God required, Cain got angry with God and jealous of Abel who brought the required sacrifice that was acceptable to God. That is just like a lot of us in the body of Christ today. We know what God requires of us. God said that He would write His commandments upon our hearts. For those of us who profess to be born again, He has done just that. We know by the inward witness of the Holy Spirit when we are stepping out of line. But we do our thing anyway and blame God when bad things happen to us while we are doing our own thing. Just like Cain who killed his brother out of jealousy, God forgives us and bears with us because His love suffers long. Yes, there is always a consequence to pay. God said the wages of sin is death. But just like He held back death and did not just slay Cain doing to him what he did to his brother, even more so today God holds back death and does not slay us and do to us what we do to others. The story of Hosea is an excellent example of God's long-suffering love.

The word of the Lord that came unto Hosea, the son of Beeri, in the days of Uzziah, Jotham, Ahaz, and Hezekiah, kings of Judah, and in the days of Jeroboam the son of Joash, King of Israel. The beginning of the word of the Lord by Hosea, and the Lord said to Hosea, Go, take unto thee a wife of whoredoms and children of whoredoms: for the land hath committed great whoredom, departing from the Lord. So he went and took Gomer the daughter of Diblaim; which conceived, and bare him a son... And she conceived again, and bare a daughter, and

*God said unto him, call her name Lo-ruhamah...
Now when she had weaned Lo-ruhamah, she conceived again and called his name Lo-ammi. (Hos.
1:1–3, 6, 8–9)*

God told Hosea to marry a prostitute as a symbolic representation of the sin and idolatry of their nation and to show the people
Israel and Judah just how much He loved them and would receive
them if they would repent of their sins, put away their idol worship,
and return to Him and worship Him alone.

Hosea married Gomer who bore three children of which only
the firstborn was Hosea's. In verse 3 it states, "She bore him a son."
This is the only time that it says that. The next two children were conceived from Gomer's adulterous affairs. The name of the first child
born in adultery, Loruhamah, meant "no mercy" and represented the
coming judgment upon Israel. The name of the second child born in
adultery, Loammi, meant not my people and resented the condition
of the children of Judah and Israel and the fact that they had gone so
far away from Him that they were no longer His people and He was
no longer their God. Repeatedly Gomer went back out to the life of
prostitution in spite of having a husband that loved and provided for
her and brought back to Hosea the fruits of her sin.

Likewise, we come to church, a building, an edifice professing
Christ, but run back out to the world seeking the lust of our flesh,
lust of our eyes, and the pride of life not considering the love which
God has shown us through Jesus Christ and the sacrifice of His only
Son for our sins. But most church attendees take it even further and
attempt to hide their sin and become hypocrites who judge others
while backbiting, gossiping, and criticizing them. I usually hear the
latest gossip about the fallacies of other ministries from the pulpit
first. I have yet to hear someone speaking of other ministries' failures,
at the time it is mentioned have everyone in the audience stand up,
and pray for that ministry and its leaders. Hosea continued to go
after Gomer, patiently enduring her whoredom as a demonstration
of God's love for us and His patient endurance of our sin. What do

you think would happen if the body of Christ would follow Hosea's lead and do what Paul said to the Galatians?

> *Brethren, if a man be overtaken in a fault,*
> *ye which are spiritual, restore such and one in the*
> *spirit of meekness; considering thyself, lest thou also*
> *be tempted.* (Gal. 6:1–2)

The key to this scripture is "ye which are spiritual." Far too many members of the body of Christ today are not grounded in the word of God and have no idea what it means to be spiritual. So many of us profess Christ, but we either do not know Him or do not spend enough time with Him to allow Him to change us into His image. Romans 5:5 says His Holy Spirit, which is given unto us, sheds the love of God abroad in our hearts. The Amplified version says that God's love has been poured out in our heart. God is love. What He is has been poured out into us. Therefore, we have the same ability to do for others what He has done for us. We have the same ability to suffer long with others as God does with us. But far too many people in the body of Christ either forgot this scripture is in the Bible or have never taken time to read to know that it is there. Gossip, backbiting, pride, arrogance, deceit, deception, fornication, adultery, perversion, and many other likes prevail in the body of Christ. Those that do these things are the very ones who look down the barrel of their nose at others who have faults and weaknesses just like their own but say you are supposed to just give up on others. My question to all those who judge others without first judging themselves is, where would you be if God through Jesus Christ had given up on you? No, you do not drink alcohol or take drugs. No, you do not commit adultery. However, you are a fornicator. You lie, you steal, you backbite, you are full of pride and arrogance, and you rejoice when you see other church leaders struggle with shortcomings. What if God had given up on you while you were dead in your trespasses and sins? What if God did not suffer long with you when you were wallowing in your mess? Would you be alive and able to read the words of this book today? But love suffers long, even for you.

> *Yet the number of the children of Israel shall be as the sand of the sea, which cannot be measured nor numbered; and it shall come to pass, that in the place where it was said unto them, Ye are not my people, there it shall be said unto them, ye are the sons of the living God. Then shall the children of Judah and the children of Israel be gathered together, and appoint themselves one head, and they shall come up out of the land: for great shall be the day of Jezreel.* (Hos. 1:10–11)

God turned from His wrath and restored Judah and Israel speaking blessing and unity over them, and He expects us to do the same for those amongst us needing to be restored. After all, love suffers long.

A word from God:

> *Love, the second great commandment is for all people to obey it, to walk in the light of it. It is not for a time but for eternity. To do My will is to love Me and to love all that I create. Loving Me means obeying me. If you do not love Me, you will not obey Me. You will not even hear me, for I speak to love. Love Me right by doing what I say, and I will bless you and your house forever. Teach this to My people.*

> *Love, Dad*

3

Love Is Kind

Charity suffereth long and is kind.

—1 Corinthians 13:4

There are five New Testament words translated kind. In this verse of scripture, the word is *chresteuomai*, which actually means "to show oneself useful." In other words, love suffers long or endures patiently and is kind or remains useful and employable. All other words translated kind in the New Testament are used as adjectives, and we know that adjectives describe the noun. *Chresteuomai* is the only word translated "kind" that is used to show action. The God kind of love shows action. In fact, it requires action to be expressed. What might have happened or what might my family's life had been like if the church members would have been long-spirited and forbearing and remained useful and serviceable to my mother in spite of her faults and shortcomings. I often wondered what would have been the case if someone from the church had visited my house and encouraged my mother to continue to come to church once she was able to get away from my father.

Far too many times people in the church or those who believe themselves to be righteous forget that Jesus had to die for them too. Church folk forget that John 3:16 says, "For God so loved the world, that He gave His only begotten Son, that whosoever believes in Him should not perish, but have everlasting life." Whosoever means you, me, my mother, your mother, and anybody else who believes. Jesus died for us all, and the love that drove Him to Calvary is unconditional. God has suffered long with man, giving up His only Son so that He can have many sons, and the two greatest commandments He gave us is to love God with all our heart, mind, and strength and to love our neighbors as ourselves. Then the apostle Paul gives us this great revelation on love in 1 Corinthians 13 to help us understand the magnitude of love and its creative ability. It is the fourth dimension of man that gives him the ability to produce substance and call things into being. Love is the creative stuff that adds substance to our faith. It is seen in our eyes, our expressions. It is heard in our voices and felt in the warmth of our countenance when it is expressed toward others.

For three years I volunteered in the nursery at my church. I usually had charge of the children eighteen to twenty-four months old, and when they were brought to my classroom, they did not always want to be there. I had to be creative and do things, to first gain their attention and then show them that they were safe with me and it was okay to be there. I would use colorful toys with lights or that made noise to attract their attentions, but the main thing I did was to hold them, cuddle them, and tell them I loved them too and show them all the love that I would show to my own child. I was not always able to calm them, but most of the time I was able to calm their crying and convince them to stay with me and the rest of the children. On one of these occasions, Israeli parents brought their child who did not know a bit of English. Yet the love of God flowing from me to this child not only stopped his crying and made him want to stay with me but also made him understand my every move concerning him whether it was feeding him cookies, changing his diaper, or setting him aside for a minute to attend to one of the other children. Letting the love of God flow from me to him made him so receptive that he was willing to be set aside for a moment and patiently wait for me to attend to another child and come back to him. He understood the language of love. That is exactly what God does for each of us. His love for us calms our fears, quiets our tears, and makes us able to wait patiently for Him. He placed His love in our hearts when we were born again, which makes us able to comfort others in the same way that He has comforted us. Remember, this love is unconditional; it has no basis, it exist for all of us regardless to our condition or position in life, and we who are children of God are required to show it to all men.

I have had many opportunities to not be forbearing and remain useful and serviceable to people in every church that I have attended. Initially I would become withdrawn and simply back away from attending. This is what I did at the Baptist church of my youth. I did not know how to walk in love because it was never taught or demonstrated to me. So rather than endure the difficulties and remain in fellowship, I fought back and stopped attending.

I remember the first Pentecostal church that I attended. I resisted God initially while questioning Him as to whether He really meant for me to go the "that church." I knew some of the people that attended that church, and I knew that some were drug users, fornicators, adulterers, and the likes. I asked God, "How am I supposed to learn to live right in *that church*?" Earlier that year I had broken off a relationship where I was living with a married man. I knew the relationship was wrong from the very beginning. But I allowed my need for financial support to override my good judgment just as a lot of live-in couples do. Nevertheless, God never rested in His love for me, and His loving-kindness continued to draw me to Him. I became so miserable in this ungodly relationship that I had to break it off.

Encounter of Love

After breaking up with this man, I was praying for a church home where I could get to a place of knowing God better and learn how to live for him. On Mother's Day, I visited a charismatic church with my sister and her boyfriend. I will never forget the reception that we received. We were an hour late, but there were still brothers in the parking lot waiting to park our car for us. There were greeters at the door and ushers waiting to show us adults to a seat and take the children to children's church. This was my first time being in a charismatic atmosphere. Praise and worship was still going on. There was a man behind me that was jumping, clapping, and yelling praises to the Lord. I wondered what on earth was that all about. I was not used to this kind of environment. I found out later that this man had fathered twins when doctors had told him that he would never father any children. When the doctors had given him a bad report he turned to the church and faith in God and in God's word. Now he was celebrating what God could do.

As I turned back around from observing this young man, a woman dancing in the spirit came and pulled me into the isle and do-si-doed me a few times. Before I knew it, the spirit fell in that church, and we were ushered into an aura of worship that I had never known before. The church was divided into four sections that seated approximately one hundred people in each section. I sat in an inside aisle seat in the fourth section. Suddenly, there appeared a woman at the front of my section speaking a language that I did not understand. She spoke in this language and then spoke in English alternately. I was totally amazed with this woman because she was walking back and forth, up and down (I realized later that it was the pattern of the cross) without bumping into anyone even though her eyes were tightly shut. I was so mesmerized that I could not take my eyes off her. I looked around at everyone around me, and all the other people except one man had their heads bowed and eyes closed. However, I could not close my eyes; I had to see this strange thing. What language was that, and how in the world could this woman walk back and forth, up and down like that with her eyes tightly shut and never bump into anyone? Suddenly she stopped and leaned into the face of the man that was also watching her, and at that very moment, it dawn on me what she was saying. "How long shall I bear you, how long must I suffer you? Repent, repent, fornication, whoremongering, drugs, drunkenness. My children, how long must I bear you, how long must I put up with you? Repent, Repent." She turned from him and came straight to me, leaned into my face, and said, "My child, how long must I suffer you? How long shall I bear you? Fornication, whoremongering, drugs, drunkenness, repent, repent." I looked the woman square in the face as she spoke to me, her eyes tightly closed so that she could not possibly see me. Then she began to speak in that language again, and I became so convicted that all I could do was drop my head and say, "Forgive me, Lord." I had no doubt that was God speaking to me through that woman, and I knew He was telling me to clean up my life. Even though I was a backslidden wretch, God's loving-kindness reached out to me through the people of this church to draw me back to Him.

I have looked back on that day many times over the past twenty-five years. One of the times that I was reminiscing that day the Lord spoke to me and told me, "I said My child because I had not let go of you yet." No, instead of letting go of me, the Lord was patient and long-suffering toward me and showed me kindness through the love of this body of believers. Instead of shunning me, He drew me to Him. Instead of meanness, He showed me loving-kindness through the love of these people and that made me set my heart to change my ways and learn how to live for Him. I left that church feeling like I mattered to God and to those people. They were so far away from my home, and I did not have my own transportation, so I knew this could not be my church home. But I was even more determined to find a place where I could learn how to live right. This time I remembered to find a dictionary and look up all of those words including the ones where I thought I already knew what they meant. Yet I still questioned God concerning "that church" that God was leading me to. I was more determined to learn how to live right, but I was still forgetting that I had to be forgiven for stuff just like the people in "that church."

Love suffers long and remains patient and kind, useful and employable so that God can use the one operating in this God kind of love to draw sinners and backsliders like me back to Him. He is not partial, and there are no big sins or little sins. It is all sin, and we all need a body of Christ with those who will suffer long and be kind to all who enter in while we are being changed into His image. That Pentecostal church that God led me to was the beginning of true spiritual growth. Yes, I had trouble. But there were those who showed me the patience and kindness that I needed to stay put and grow in grace through the love of God flowing from them to me.

A word from God:

October 20, 1998

This is how I operate in the earth. I pick others up through you. I save others through you. If you do not obey Me, I cannot work. If I cannot work through you, I will no longer tolerate you. I need My vessels to obey Me, to worship Me, and to praise Me. When others see you worshiping Me and praising Me, it will provoke them. It will convict them. It will draw them to me. I love all My creation, and I do not desire to lose anything to the devil. My purpose is to save, preserve, set free, deliver, and restore all to our Father in heaven.

Work while it is day, for the night comes when no man can work, and many there be that stand in the wrong way right now, some in the church and some in the world. Feed My flock that I have given you. Do it with simplicity and honor. Don't stray in any way. I will be with you in all I send you to do. Others may not like the task that I have given you to do, but you have been faithful, and your reward is forthcoming.

Enjoy, but don't forget who blessed you.

Dad

4

Love Does Not Envy

Charity suffereth long and is kind; charity envieth not.

—1 Corinthians 13:4

Envieth—(2206) *zeloo /dzay-lo'-o/,* to have warmth of feeling for or against; zealously affect, but not well. Love does not zealously affect others in a bad way.

Envy is the first on the list of things that love does not do, and rightfully so. It seems that all other opposition, all other harshness, all other things that lead to strife starts with envy. Envy is misplaced zeal. It is the deep desire to affect something or someone but not in a good way. Envy is often called the green-eyed monster; however, most people's eyes do not turn green when they are filled with envy. But you can hear it in their voices, not just in what they say but in the tone of how they say it. The urge to backbite and gossip about others starts with negative feelings about what other people possess or the position or status that other people hold.

Proverbs 3:31 says, "Envy not the oppressor, and chose none of his way." The Amplified version says, "Do not resentfully envy and be jealous of an unscrupulous, grasping man, and choose none of his ways." Why? Because an unscrupulous man is willing to do anything, say anything to get by or to obtain riches and status. An unscrupulous man will literally sell his soul to hell and do anything to anybody to gain money, wealth, and status, never once looking back to see and consider the people that he hurt and trample on or the damnation that he brings on himself for the wrong that he do. Many of these are in the church.

I had a brother that died young when he was only twenty-four years old. Before he died, he had secured an apartment and let one of my cousins move in with him. That cousin envied everything about my brother: his clothes, his friends, his accomplishments, girlfriend—everything. When my brother died, my family and I went through his apartment looking for a certain beige-colored three-piece suit that my brother wore. We could not find it anywhere, so we looked for other nice suits that Sunny had worn and could not find any of them. All we could find was a not-so-attractive green suit he wore when he first started a training program. Sunny had finished a training program, started working on a job, and purchased other nicer suits for a more professional polished look on his new job. A few weeks after we buried my brother, some of his friends came and told us that they saw our cousin wearing Sunny's clothes, particularly the beige suit that we could not find. Well, we decided not to approach my cousin or say anything to him about it because we knew that no good would come to someone who would rob the dead like that. Sure enough, barely six months later that cousin was in a severe car accident, nearly lost his life, and had to learn to walk all over again. While my cousin was going through the healing process, he came and apologize for stealing from my brother and stripping Sunny's apartment the way that he had done. Did my cousin's actions cause the accident? No, it did not. It just opened up the door for the enemy to bring havoc to his own life. All of this because of envy. Proverbs 14:30 says that envy is the rottenness of the bones. The life of the body is in the blood, and the blood is created in the bones. Rotten bones create rotten blood, and rotten blood brings death to the body. Bad blood in the body is synonymous to envy in the heart and soul of man.

> *Let not thine heart envy sinners: but be thou*
> *in the fear of the Lord all the day long.* (Prov. 23:17
> KJV)

*Let not your heart envy sinners, but continue
in the reverent and worshipful fear of the Lord all
the day long.* (AMP)

There is scripture throughout the Bible that gives guidance concerning envy. In this verse of Proverbs, the writer is telling us to continue in reverence and fear of God because in this state of mind, we will remain close to Him and not concern ourselves with what the sinners appear to have going on for them. In this state of mind, we will also not be jealous of what our brothers and sisters in Christ possess. It is truly only appearance. If you spend some time with sinners who appear to have so much going good for them, you will find that it is not at all as good as it is made out to be. I tell you there is nothing worse than having a lot of money and people there to help you spend it who leave when the money is gone. In addition, because sinners do not know or fear God, they have no idea what their end will be and the simple fact that their earthly wealth and status cannot save them from the wrath of God. The word of God tells us to not be envious of evil men and don't keep company with them because all their minds do is search out, devise, and plot destruction for others. If that be the case with envy, how can we honestly and properly show the love of God to any man if we are envious of them?

If you spend time with brothers and sisters that are living for God and being blessed in their living, something could rub off on you. You could come to know God like they know God and be blessed in your fellowship with godly people, but not if you are envious of them. It is written that for envy, the people delivered Jesus to be crucified. The people saw the power, influence, and wealth that Jesus had. They saw how those that surrendered their life to Him gave and poured out their all to Him, and they envied that. None of the good that Jesus did mattered to the people that betrayed Him. A heart full of envy does not see or care about the good that causes the manifestation of wealth and status. It does not dare put forth the positive energy and effort required to attain that which is envied. All that a heart full of envy see is what others have that it does not.

It amazes me to see the effect of envy in the church and especially among leaders. It often seems as if the quest for saving souls is not simply because the leader wants to save a soul from hell. It seems that some pastors' primary quest is to increase their numbers to compete with churches larger than theirs. Some evangelists want to be able to count the number of souls that come up for salvation to compete with another evangelist that has saved many souls. I have even heard one pastor challenge his congregation to get out there and get the people into church so they can tear down the five-thousand-seat sanctuary that they have and build a thirty-thousand-seat sanctuary. So then the quest ceased to be the love of God seeking to save soul but the lust of envy to compete with what another ministry has.

The Amplified version of 1 Corinthians 13:4 says, "Love never is envious nor boil over with jealousy." Love is always happy to see another succeed, have good things, and prosper. A person walking in the God kind of love who can be happy for and contribute to another person's success is a person that invites the power of God to work in and through his life.

5

Love Does Not Vaunt Itself

*Charity suffereth long and is kind; charity
envieth not; charity vaunteth not itself.*

—*1 Corinthians 13:4*

*Let another man praise thee, and not thine own
mouth; a stranger, and not thine own lips.*

—*Proverbs 27:2*

The word translated *vaunteth* means to boast one's self or to give a self-display. It refers to a person who uses embellishing words and symbolic trimmings to dress up who they are exclusively. Lying comes easily for people who boast and brag about themselves. Use and abuse of others is just an everyday thing. People who exalt themselves tend to have an exaggerated idea of who they are but then surround themselves with the people who have the talent and skills that they lack. When it is required to give a demonstration of who they profess to be, the person who boasts of himself will use those other people to create their display and act as if that which is presented is innately them when it is not. This person is often mean, rude, and harsh to others who actually possess the talent, skill, or ability.

People who vaunt themselves often make a bold display as if they care but never really show the God kind of love to anyone because they are too busy doting on themselves. This person constantly sings his or her own praise about their eye view of their accomplishment. They love to show off their knowledge, possessions, and accomplishments. But they never give any recognition to anyone else, not even God. Jesus Himself said that without Him, we can do nothing. Yet I have even heard one preacher say that statement is unscriptural. How many times have I turned on the television and heard preachers telling their stories of how they got somebody saved or got somebody healed or cast the devil out of this one or that one. The problem with this type of attitude is no consideration is given to what it took to get that unsaved person to church and all the prayers that went out preparing that fallow ground to receive the words of life that leads to salvation. In 1 Corinthians 3:6, Paul made a statement to the people of Corinth that applies here and in every work of the ministry. He said, "I have planted, Apollos watered; but God gave the increase." This is true in every work of ministry. A seed had to be sown and the planting has to grow to fruition before there can be a harvest. Equating everything good to myself as if I alone make everything happen is deluding myself. This, my friend, is a dangerous place to be because this is where those who respond this way begin to cross the threshold of claiming God's glory and exalting themselves above God.

> *It is not good to eat much honey; so for men to seek glory, their own glory, causes suffering and not glory.* (Prov. 25:27 AMPC)

The amplified version of this scripture gives us a better understanding of what it means to praise and extol one's self exclusively. This type of behavior causes others to suffer because in most cases, the persons praising themselves are claiming credit for the work of another while denying wages or benefits to the one who actually produced the work.

Romans 12:3 gives good guidance to all who are tempted to step out of love in this fashion, and the Amplified version says it best:

> *For by the grace (unmerited favor of God) given to me I warn everyone among you not to estimate and think of himself more highly than he ought [not to have an exaggerated opinion of his own importance], but to rate his ability with sober judgment, each according to the degree of faith apportioned by God to him.*

If we would apply this principle to our lives daily, there would be no big I's and little yous in the body of Christ. This is the key right here. It is those who think more highly of themselves than they ought who boast and brag about who they are or take themselves to be. This is not a matter of showing confidence as some might say. David had and showed confidence in God while he was on the backside of the mountain tending sheep after he had been anointed as king. That confidence came out of him when he saw Goliath, but until then, no one knew it was there. It was not until David's father Jesse asked him to take some food to his brothers on the battlefield and got a chance to hear Goliath taunting the army of Israel that provoked David to speak out what was in him. David got angry. I call this righteous indignation. He asked, "Who is this uncircumcised Philistine who defies the army of the loving God?" You see, David knew his God and was confident in what God would do based on what He had already done. David had great confidence in what God would do and what he was able to do because of God. This was not bragging; this was simply speaking out and acting on his confidence in God, all the while giving God the glory. He did not say what he had or what he would do until he first stated what God had already done.

This is an excellent example of the kind of humility that is required to overcome the temptation to boast and brag about ourselves and our accomplishments. Putting God first puts the focus where it should be, and when the focus is where it should be, then the love of God shines in us and through us.

6

Love Is Not Puffed Up

Charity suffereth long and is kind; charity envieth not;
charity vaunteth not itself, is not puffed up.

—1 Corinthians 13:4

Pride goeth before destruction and an
haughty spirit before and fall.

—Proverbs 16:18

The Greek word translated *puffed* is *phusioo*, and its primary meaning refers to that which is blown up or inflated, and it is used metaphorically in the New Testament in the sense of being puffed up with pride.

This area seems to weigh down the greatest portion of the body of Christ. Pride is a butt kicker for the average person. It is especially so for those in high-profile positions like those in the fivefold ministry, musicians (successful musicians), deacons, lay leaders, or anyone in positions of authority. It is an avenue that leads to destruction for all who will not judge themselves. If you listen to most prideful people who go around bragging about themselves and their accomplishment, they always seem to misquote Proverbs 16:18. They usually say, "Pride goes before a fall." That is not what the Bible says. I believe there is a definite distinction between pride and haughty in this scripture reference. You see, a person could experience a single moment of success and become haughty about it. Then some other situation comes, and that person could experience a moment of failure that overshadows that success. That failure causes the haughty person to fall, which rounds him out and brings him back down to earth, so to speak.

However, people full of pride has had many successes and have gotten caught up in who they think they are and forgot all about God and those that were sent to help him or her to be successful. All of a sudden it is I, me, my, and nobody else. In most cases, I have found that most people who go around boasting about themselves and tooting their own horn are lacking something in their life but don't want anyone else to know that they are lacking. But their success has made them to become so full of themselves that they manage to delude themselves into thinking that they are all of that and a bag of chips all by themselves with no help from anybody, not even God. I have even heard one preacher tell a story about a situation that only God could have made him to know and then ask the audience how they thought he knew it. When no one responded, the preacher said, "My spirit told me," and left it at that. I wanted to ask where his spirit got it from, but out of respect for authority, I held my tongue. But I often wondered, was it so hard to say, "God told me," or, "The Holy Spirit revealed it to me"? This is a very dangerous place to be. Because before you know it, that man or that woman begins to steal God's glory, and stealing from God is what leads to the path of destruction.

When Pride Was All I Had

Years ago, whenever I spoke about my life and the hard times that I experienced growing up and as a single parent, I used to say pride was all I had. Then I came to know God and the word of God better and what the Bible said about pride. I realized pride was all I had because I had it. In other words, because I had so much pride, there was no room for me to have anything else. God could not give me any of the things that I needed because He could not get me to move past all the pride that I had to open up and tell somebody what I needed.

For example, I was in my third year of a two-year college. It was the end of the first quarter of the third year, and I was repeating several classes that I had already taken during my first year but scored poorly on them. When I got ready to go to college, I did not seek counseling for establishing my curriculum. I knew what I wanted to do and did not feel that I need anybody to tell me what I needed to do. I took the required tests for English and Math and did not feel that I needed to get any additional counseling. I knew I wanted to own a nightclub restaurant where people could come dine and eat good food with a dance floor for those who loved to dance. I wanted live entertainment, and I was going to MC all my shows. So I figured I needed to know business, so I signed up for business classes, and I needed to know music, so I signed up for music classes. I love music and always wanted to play the piano, so this was right down my alley.

I was foolish enough to think that I could combine two curriculums without knowing that is what I was doing because I was too prideful to seek counseling concerning my classes. At the end of the first year, I had decent grades in music classes that would not bring employment and low grades and withdrawals in business classes that would lead to employment. So there I was at the end of the first quarter of the third year getting the kind of grades that made two of my instructors take a closer look at me. They were both women, and women are very perceptive. One of them was the head of the department with the kind of connections that could open doors for me. They both could see that I had financial issues. They knew that I was a single parent, and they knew that I was one of the low-income welfare students that had to wait for grant money to arrive to obtain needed school supplies including the very important class textbooks. My instructors were reviewing the two Ds and an F that was replaced with two As and a B and were now seeking to know my actual status and how they could help me. But pride was all I had, and it was all I left me with. Because while I was saying all I had was pride, the truth is all I had was fear and shame, and I was too ashamed to let these two ladies who wanted to help me know my situation. I simply soaked up their accolades of how well I had done; after all, I knew I had it in me. I knew I was smart, but I also knew that I had needed of some other things that would help me be a better student. But out of pride, I dared not reveal my true needs to them and simply settled for the accolades of my momentary accomplishment.

Pride for some is an exaggerated display of perceived accomplishments, and for others, like me, it is a mask to hide the shame and inferiority of that which we lack. Either way, we use words to embellish and exalt ourselves and miss the true love of God in both giving and receiving. We all need to receive love. Let me say that again. We all need to receive love. But when we get over into pride and get blown up and inflated about ourselves and who we think we are, we miss out on the opportunity to receive the love that God has for us. We also fail to sow the love of God into others so there tends to be a limitation in the love that we receive.

There is another side of pride where those that operate in it may not be aware of what they are doing. It is the side that gives God the glory and credit for most things like healing and prosperity, but when asked a question about a matter, the person operating in this type of pride will give their opinion and never once ask God what He has to say about it or even consult one scripture.

I was watching a Christian TV program where a pastor was conducting a panel discussion. This pastor is well-known for his words of wisdom which is why he receives so much attention from people needing answers to their problems. However, this day was not the case. A woman had written in and asked about childbearing after age forty. The woman had graduated from high school and gone straight to college. After graduating from college, she chose to pursue a career and financial stability before entering into marriage and starting a family. Now at the age of forty-two, she had met someone she wanted to marry and was wondering about having children at her age. I was surprised to hear the pastor's response to her question. His only words (at least on the air) was his opinion which was totally opposite to the woman's desire. Because he and his wife did not want to have any more children after forty, he passed his feelings on to the woman asking the question and offered nothing from God or the word of pertaining to children and families. As I sat there listening, several scriptures came to my mind about what God's word says about childbearing:

> *And he shall be like a tree planted by the rivers of water, that bringeth forth his fruit in his season; his leaf also shall not wither; and whatsoever he doeth shall prosper.* (Ps 1:3)

> *The righteous shall flourish like the palm tree: he shall grow like a cedar in Lebanon. Those that be planted in the house of the Lord shall flourish in the courts of our God. They shall still bring forth fruit in old age; they shall be flat and flourishing; to show that God is upright: He is my rock, and there is no unrighteousness in Him.* (Ps 92:12–15)

> *Lo, children are an heritage of the Lord and the fruit of the womb is his reward.* (Ps. 127:3)

> *Let not a widow be taken into the number under threescore [sixty] years old having been the wife of one man…but the younger widows refuse: for when they have begun to wax wanton against Christ, they will marry… I will therefore that the younger women [under sixty] marry, bear children, guide the house, give none occasion to the adversary to speak reproachfully.* (1 Tim. 5:9–14)

This is just a few of the scriptures that readily came to mind as I listened to this program. I know that this pastor did not mean any harm to the woman with the question. However, if that woman's faith and desire was not strong enough to continue to seek God on the matter, then she probably went away discouraged and never received the family that she desired. It is never enough to give people our opinion without first searching out God's word on the matter.

Those who think themselves worthy to give their opinion and never consult God's word on the matter are doing both themselves and the one receiving their counsel and injustice. The agape love of God would not have let this woman who loves Him and desire to please Him go away empty. No, pride did that.

God Resist the Proud

But He gives more grace. Wherefore he saith, God resisteth the proud, but giveth grace unto the humble. (Jas. 4:6)

But He gives us more and more grace (power of the Holy Spirit, to meet this evil tendency and all others fully). That is why He says, God sets Himself against the proud and haughty, but gives grace [continually] to the lowly (those who are humble enough to receive it). (AMPC)

I had read this scripture many times, but it was one of Joyce Meyer's teachings that brought my attention to this scripture. Of all the things we encounter in life, this is the primary area where men mess up and God says that He sets Himself against it. When we walk in pride, we hurt ourselves by opening up unwanted doors to hardships and situations that we cannot handle. We hurt others by the way we handle them, and we invite the resistance of God so that when we want or need to be blessed, when we want or need God to intervene on our behalf, He will not because of our position of pride. When we operate in pride, we step out of love and invite unwanted events in our life. No, love is not puffed up and inflated with pride, and those who operate in pride operate outside of the will of God.

This by far is one of the most dangerous areas of a Christian's life as far as God is concerned. You see, when we get puffed up and over into pride, we lose insight from God. The Holy Spirit cannot show us anything because we are too full of ourselves and into the natural to receive revelation from God. The scripture explicitly states that the natural man cannot receive the things of the Spirit of God because they are foolishness to him. He cannot even know them because they are spiritually discerned (1 Cor. 2:14). When we are puffed up and inflated with pride, we cannot receive true direction from God. I have seen several situations where ministers of the gospel were derailed because of pride. In one situation, God had given the minister direction concerning a wife and concerning governing leadership to aid him in his ministry. But that minister chose to go his own way. Even when things got so hard, members started straying, and the church ceased growing; the minister stated that he knew he was wrong, "but sometimes you go so far that you cannot turn back." Only pride would stop you from turning back when you see eminent destruction looming ahead of you. Proverbs 22:3 says, "A prudent man foreseeth the evil, and hideth himself: but the simple pass on, and are punished." That minister had said over and over how the Lord wanted him to take that city for God. I believed that was true because that was what I had been praying for many years. But today, after twenty years of pasturing, not only is that minister no longer in that city, but he also can hardly be found and has moved locations many times. The ministry that was initially growing dwindled down to a few family members.

In another situation, the pastor who God had placed in charge of several vital ministries received and application from a woman who was interested in a leadership position in one of those ministries. The pastor received the woman and placed her in a position of authority above other leadership that had been on staff for years and had been his staunchest supporters. Inside one year that woman had wreaked havoc in the area she was assigned, so much that the lead elder and his wife decided to resign the position that they held and leave the church. In a ceremony, the pastor described his initial experience with this woman and stated that as he was holding her resume in his hand and was reviewing her credentials, inside of one hour she was elevated from a mere applicant to as it were a comrade. He went on to say that anyone opposing her also opposed him.

I asked God, what kind of bewitchment is that? How is it that a pastor who supposedly has so much revelation and insight from

God could be so blinded by this woman? God told me pride had blinded him. He had become so puffed up in whom he was and lost sight of who God was in him that he could not see the deception of the woman. Had it not been for the prayers of the saints interceding for this pastor and the leadership that had determined it was time to leave, that pastor would never have woken up out of his blinded stupor.

Love is not puffed up. Love is ever open to receive wisdom and direction from God. In 1 John 2:10 it says, "He that loves his brother abides in the light, and there is no occasion of stumbling in him." Love, God's love in us overrides the blindness of pride and helps us to humble ourselves under His mighty hand so that we can show His love to all who cross our path. Then we become shining lights that draw others to him.

7

Love Does Not Behave Unseemly

Charity suffereth long, and is kind;
charity envieth not; charity vaunteth not itself, is not puffed up,
Doth not behave itself unseemly.

—*1 Corinthians 13:4–5*

The Greek word translated *unseemly* is *aschemosune*, pronounced *as-kay-mos-oo'-nay* and more accurately means improper, indecency, shame, and nakedness. It is necessary to have a full understanding of the use of this word because it is an act or behavior that is used extensively by every member of the body of Christ without regard to level or position. When we behave unseemly, we cause people to be disturbed or to have painful feelings of guilt, incompetence, indecency, or blameworthiness. Adam and Eve were naked and not ashamed when they were first created. However, when they entered into sin, their eyes were open, and they knew that they were naked and were ashamed. Therefore, it is safe to say that anything that is indecent—that brings shame and causes the feeling of nakedness—is unseemly and an act of sin. This is a very broad category and can be applied to everything the other categories do not address. Sin brings shame. For the perpetrator, that is rightfully so. But what about the victim? That is the key point about this step out of love. For example, gossiping is not envy, although it could be a result of envy. Lying is not boasting, but it usually what people do when they are boasting. The primary purpose of gossipers or liars is to malign, disparage, degrade, or somehow weaken the status or position of another, and that is unseemly and a step outside of the realm of love. The word of God has much to say about gossiping and lying.

The first scripture that deals with gossiping is found in Leviticus and is referred to as talebearing:

> *Thou shalt not go up and down as a talebearer among thy people: neither shalt thou stand against the blood of thy neighbor: I am the Lord.* (Lev. 19:16)

> *You shall not go up and down as a dispenser of gossip and scandal among your people, nor shall you [secure yourself by false testimony or by silence and] endanger the life of your neighbor. I am the Lord.* (AMPC)

A better translation of talebearer in this version of scripture is scandal-monger and refers to one who travels about carrying tales. This may not seem like a problem to those who walk in this light, and I have heard many justify their action by saying, "I just thought you needed to know," or, "Pray for so-and-so." The fact is some people just cannot seem to keep their nose out of other men's matters. On the surface, gossipers do not appear to be the least affected by the situation that they are tattling about, and they never stop to see if there is any truth to the matter. But the fact of the matter is that gossipers, liars, and evildoers hurt them just as much as they hurt others. They just do not see the harvest that they reap right away. But God watches over His word to perform it, and we as the body of Christ should be aware of all of God's word and not just what we want to speak over ourselves for our own selfish desires. I have always used the following scriptures to remind myself that any snare that I set for others will catch me instead and vice versa.

> *Whoso diggeth a pit shall fall therein: and he that rolleth a stone, it will return upon him [marginal notation, "roll back on him"].* (Prov. 26:27)

Whoso causeth the righteous to go astray in an evil way, he shall fall himself into his own pit: but the upright shall have good things in possession. (Prov. 28:10)

Be not deceived; God is not mocked: for whatsoever a man soeth, that shall he also reap. (Gal. 6:7)

Let us not therefore judge one another anymore: but judge this rather, that no man put a stumbling block or an occasion to fall in his brother's way. (Rom. 14:13)

I remember my first experience dealing with gossip in the church. I had just joined my first Pentecostal church. I love music and would set in the pews and sing along with the choir if I knew the song. One Sunday the minister in charge of the choir announced the choir was looking for new members and anyone interested should come to choir practice on Thursday. My sister and I decided to go to the choir practice to audition for the choir. It was a cold day in February, and I decided to go straight from work to the church. I wore a silk plaid skirt that came below my knees, a cream white blouse, and a blue Nehru velour jacket under my winter coat. The church was an old movie theater, and the seats were the same old rows of connected movie chairs, so I decided to sit on the same side with the choir only a few rows back so I could see how well my voice blended with them. I will never forget the songs that they were practicing because they were singing what was in my heart. "When the battle is over, we shall wear a crown in the New Jerusalem," and "Jesus, I love You for your tender care. Jesus, I love You, I'll own you anywhere. Jesus, Jesus, I love You. Oh, yes I do."

There were already so many people on the choir. I did not understand why they needed more people, and my voice was so rusty. I had not sung in the choir since I was a child. My sisters and I used to sing ourselves to sleep at night. My oldest sister was the lead singer because she was the oldest, and she knew all the verses to the songs that we sang in our Baptist church. My grandmother and aunt sang in the choir every Sunday, and my sisters and I sang when the children's choir sung. So needless to say, I was looking forward to singing in this choir, but apparently this was not the time.

It was cold when we arrived, so I wrapped my coat tightly around me as I sat down. The heat was on, but it had not warmed up yet. While the minister and the choir director was speaking to the choir, I sunk down and lay back in my chair and began to pray and talk to God, thanking Him for saving me and bringing me into this church. I was asking God to bless this choir to receive my sister and me and be patient with us while our voices were reconditioned for singing. Both of us had been in the world drinking and smoking and wreaking havoc on our voices. We could still sing, but our voices were weak and raspy. I became hot, so I opened my coat but continued to talk to God. I noticed the minister come and look up the aisle at me several times and even walked up the aisle and left the sanctuary and returned a couple of times. I had no idea what was happening. I just kept praying and talking to God. Suddenly, the choir director came to the front of the aisle and started looking at me and making statements about a wicked woman, lewd woman, whore, and harlot and telling everybody to clap their hands and praise the Lord. Three times, he did this with his eyes on me the whole while. Each time I thought he sure was looking at me while he was saying that. The third time he pointed his fingers and scraped them together giving the shame-on-you signal while pointing at me. Then I realized he was talking about me, and everyone in the choir started looking at me. I examined myself to see if something was wrong with me. My skirt that was below my knees while standing was still at my knees, and my left leg was crossed over my right leg. All the buttons on my blouse was intact, so what was the problem, and why as he saying all those things pointing at me? My sister, who was sitting across the aisle in the first seat just ahead of me, was also looking back at me. I was so shocked and embarrassed that I could not move. I forgot all about my prayer to God. What had I done? Suddenly, a breeze came and brushed my legs. Then my sister got up, walked up the aisle, and whispered to me to pull my skirt down.

I jumped up, made sure that my skirt was as far down as it could go, wrapped my coat back around myself again, sat back down, and stayed there until the rehearsal was over. I was too ashamed to get up and go forward to join the choir after all of that. I had checked myself over and over when the choir director was making those negative statements about bad women, and I continued to play the whole situation over and over in my head. When my sister and I left to go home, I asked her what she saw. All she could say was my legs. I asked what she meant, "my legs." Could you see up my skirt? She said no. Could you see my slip? She said no. What did you see? Her only reply was nothing but my legs. Okay, then how much of my legs did you see? Just from the knees down. I was so hurt, ashamed, and embarrassed I vowed I would never try to join that choir again. I had to take the bus home, and all the way home and even after I arrived home, the devil kept taunting me with the words of the choir director and the looks of the minister. I had already been accused of chasing after another minister and now this. I could not get the sounds and looks out of my head. All of this took place on Thursday. The following Sunday the minister who I was accused of lusting after who was not at the rehearsal but whose turn it was to preach walked to the edge of the pulpit, looked me directly in the face, and said, "I don't blame you. If a woman sat with her legs wide open in from of me, I would look too." This time I was floored. The whole church began to gossip about, shun, and turn their nose up at me. For weeks, I tried to shake the feelings of guilt and shame but to no avail. When the people were not around to turn their nose up at me, the devil was talking to me, and somehow their actions and the devil's words caused me to lose sight of what God had said to me. Finally, I figured if I am doing that which I am not aware of because of my determination to remain celibate until God brings a godly man into my life, I needed to do something about it. I had been resisting an attractive young single man who was not a member of the body of Christ for nine months. I decided I would give in just once, relieve my frustration, and start all over again. Only this time I will already be in church and will gain strength from the word preached to help me be better this time. Needless to say, it was not just one time. I backslide into fornication and a bad relationship that ended after an abortion and two miscarriages, the last of which was my twin daughters Eshauna and Lashaunda. But God, here is a truth that most people in the church fail to realize.

> *Therefore, ye shepherds, hear the word of the Lord; As I live, saith the Lord God, surely because my flock became a prey, and my flock became meat to every beast of the field, because there was no shepherd, neither did my shepherds search for my flock, but the shepherds fed themselves, and fed not my flock; Therefore, O ye shepherds, hear the word of the Lord; Thus saith the Lord God; Behold, I am against the shepherds; and I will require my flock at their hand, and cause them to cease from feeding the flock; neither shall the shepherds feed themselves anymore; for I will deliver my flock from their mouth, that they may not be meat for them. And as for you, O my flock, thus saith the Lord God; Behold, I judge between cattle and cattle, between rams and the he goats. Seemeth it a small thing unto you to have eaten up the good pasture, but ye must tread down with your feet the residue of your pastures? And to have drunk of the deep waters, but ye must foul the residue with your feet? And as for my flock, they eat that which ye have trodden with your feet; and they drink that which ye have fouled with your feet. Therefore thus saith the Lord God unto them; Behold, I, even I, will judge between the fat cattle and between the lean cattle. Because ye have thrust with side and with shoulder, and pushed all the diseased with your horns, till ye have scattered them abroad; Therefore will I save my flock, and they shall no more be a prey; and I will judge between cattle and cattle. (Ezek. 34:7–10, 17–22)*

It is strictly my humble opinion, but it behooves all those who profess the name of Jesus Christ to get well acquainted with the entire chapter of Ezekiel 34. God says He will judge between all of us. First the negligent shepherds that are feeding off the flock but not feeding the flock and caring for them and then between the fat and lean laity. When we do harm to others and think we are getting away with it, we must know that God has His hand in the matter. He judges between all of us. He gives us all time to repent. But if we choose not to repent and continue to think that we are going to trample on that which belongs to God, we must know that there are consequences. I was in the middle of my second trimester when I miscarried my daughters. Birthing them and watching them die was by far the hardest thing that I have ever had to do. The guilt, the shame, the pain of the lost almost killed me. I wanted to die with my daughters. When I was not in church, neither of those ministers or choir members inquired about me or prayed for me. Fortunately, there were three people that inquired about me and prayed for me: the deacon, missionary, and willing worker that assisted in my baptism when I first joined the church. I was so hurt and bitter that I did not want to hear my sister tell me that they were inquiring about me and praying for me, but I am sure glad they did.

I was out of church for a year and a half. When I got back, a new choir was in place, and most of the people of the previous choir was gone. I listened to one young man that was in that choir but did not take part in the gossip as he was saying that he did not know what had happened. One minute they were a choir, and the next minute they were not. Immediately, God spoke to me and said, "I judged in the matter." God made me to know that the moment that I decided that I would never try to join that choir again, He judged that they should not come together again. The incident happened in February, and they were planning to participate in a gospel competition in April. They never made. And all who gossiped about and turned their nose up at me fell into the pit with me. In a dream I saw the minister in the pulpit who said he would look too, standing outside of a blue car and saying, "Satan come and get me," and then got in the car. Immediately Satan came and got him. He fathered a son out of wedlock that was born three months after the child that I aborted would have been born. The same was the case with every member of the choir that participated in gossiping and falsely accusing me.

God judges in matters whether we think He does or not. Many scriptures encourage us to be careful about the words that we speak. It behooves us to research them and study them. What we sow, we reap. Ditches we dig, we fall in. Stones we roll come back on us. The only way to avoid this is to take heed to our love walk and do what love would do. Love would not gossip or lie on others. No, love covers a multitude of sin. How many people have been hurt and driven out of the house of God by those who thought they were better, greater, and holier than others were? And the most prideful statement I have ever heard from the mouths of pastors and church leaders on every level is, "Just get over it." Well, tell that to God.

Pride and gossip are the tools of the spirit of Jezebel. God has used a situation that I experience in my present church to show how this spirit moves in and grows in the body of Christ. He said it is like a spider plant. Most houseplant lovers know what this is. It looks like large tuffs of grass and grows long spiky leaves just like grass. When a single tuff of spider plant is mature and strong, it sprouts a shoot that starts out as a single shoot and then splits into two, three, or four shoots. Each shoot has a baby tuff at the end. The baby tuff eventually blooms small white flowers at the top and air roots at the bottom. The flowers eventually die and turn into seedpods that dry out and drop little round black seed that grow into new plants if it falls into fertile soil. The air roots at the bottom of the sprouted tuff continue to grow and collect food and moisture from the air so that the baby tuff grows almost as big as the mother tuffs and will embed in any soil it encounters to become another large sprouting tuff. In fact, the sprout does not have to embed in soil. It will grow and mature while hanging from the mother plant and shoot spouts. Then that sprout will grow mature and shoot sprouts. I once had a hanging pot of spider plant that grew four generations of sprouts. Here is what God showed me.

The mother plant is the spirit of Jezebel working through one person sending out poisonous sprouts of gossip by speaking it to several other people. Those people lacking wisdom receive the gossip and in the process of doing so comes under the control and influence of the spirit of Jezebel. They in turn go and speak the gossip to others dropping their seeds of venomous gossip on all who receive it, and each person who receives it comes under the influence and control of the spirit of Jezebel. The whole purpose is to weaken the body of Christ and hinder the person being gossiped about from doing the work of the ministry that God has called them to do. God gave Jezebel a chance to repent, but she would not (Rev. 2:20–23). God has judged in the matter, and all who submit to the spirit of Jezebel will suffer consequences like Jezebel.

We do many other things as Christians that fall in the category of unseemly. The best way to check ourselves in this area is to stop and think about what we are about to say or what we are about to do and ask ourselves, "Would I want that said or done to me?" On the other hand, we could ask ourselves, "How would I feel if that was said or done to me?" Check to see if you would like how you would feel about what is said or done. If it would make you to have painful feelings of guilt, incompetency, or indecency; then you should know that is an unseemly act, a step out of love that must be resisted at all cost. After all, love does not behave itself unseemly.

8

Love Does Not Seek Her Own

*Charity suffereth long, and is kind; charity envieth
not; charity vaunteth not itself, is not puffed up, Doth
not behave itself unseemly, seeketh not her own.*

1 Corinthians 13:4–5

Let no man seek his own, but every man another's wealth.

1 Corinthians 10:24

*Look not every man on his own things, but
every man also on the things of others.*

Philippians 2:4

Seeketh (2212) *zeteo /dzay-teh'-o/*, to see (lit or fig.), to worship (God) (in a bad sense), to plot (against life, go about, desire to seek how to do something, or what to obtain), to seek or strive after, to require or demand.

This is a most simple yet much-misunderstood act of love. Many people think that because they are generous, they are not selfish. However, there is such a thing as being selfishly generous. In other words, you are ready to give what you are willing to give but not necessarily what a person needs or what God tells you to give. A good example of selfishness is the rich young ruler in Matthew 19. This young ruler wanted to be assured that he would inherit eternal life, so he sought Jesus to ask Him what was required. He asked Jesus, "What good thing shall I do?" because he was willing to do whatever Jesus said as long as he could agree with Jesus and it did not cost him a sacrifice. This is the key to not being selfish. Whenever we walk in selfishness, we are looking for that which gives us pleasure with no sacrifice. We look for what is going to build us up; strengthen us; make us better, wiser; and help us to shine as long as it does not cost us that which we do not want to give. The rich young ruler was willing to do the commandments because doing the commandments did not cost him anything. In fact, doing the commandments is a way of making us feel like we are somebody, like we know something and should be exalted above others because of our pious acts. But pious acts do not make us holy, just as doing the commandments did not grant the rich young ruler eternal life. If keeping the commandments could have given him what he wanted, he would not have had to ask Jesus for it.

As a child, I grew up being taught to sacrifice myself for the sake of another and God would bless me. I so desperately needed to be blessed that I would sacrifice anything that I could. We were a poor family, so I did not have money to sacrifice. Actually, money was what I needed to buy my clothes, so I would sacrifice by doing others' chores, babysitting, and running errands that no one else wanted to do. Sometimes I got paid for what I did, but most times I did not. However, I believed that if I sacrificed, God would bless me, so I sacrificed as much as any child could. The rich young ruler wanted eternal life, and I wanted earthly provisions. The question for both of us was not just what we were willing to pay for what we wanted but what we were willing to pay to prosper another. Jesus tested the rich young ruler and showed him his heart. Jesus told the rich young ruler to go and sell all that he had and give to the poor then come and follow Him. Well, the rich young ruler went away sad because he was wealthy. You see, selfishness says, "I will give what I want to give, how I want to give, where I want to give, and when I want to give, and it cannot cause me to sacrifice anything." But love is not selfish. Love gives what is needed, when it is needed, where it is needed, and how it is needed and at whatever cost or sacrifice is necessary. Love will do whatever is necessary to protect and prosper another above self.

God demonstrated His love for us by giving His only begotten Son. Jesus demonstrated his love for us by His obedience even unto death on the cross. God's love is unconditional and everlasting. It has no bias, and it is without dissimulation. Love seeks not just his own but also another man's wealth. I often wonder what would happen if churches would take down their denominational and competitive barriers and work together to save the lost. American cities have churches on every second or third block, but the neighborhood is none the better. Every pastor is looking to his own wealth, growth, and prosperity. Most pastors believe that his way is the only way, and his prophetic voice is the prophetic voice.

I once heard a popular evangelist tell a story about a preacher that was on his way to a ministry engagement and driving toward a storm. He happened to pass a very large farm where the farmer had planted wheat, and there were several farmers in combines harvesting the wheat. He stopped the one closest to him and asked what they were doing. The farmer came down from the combine to talk to him and told the preacher that there was a monster hailstorm on the horizon such as they had never seen before. The farmers did not have time to harvest all of their wheat alone, and the crops would not withstand the hailstorm. If they did not harvest now, they would not be able to harvest at all. So they all got together and decided to work together to save this one field. The farmer then excused himself to get back to the harvest of wheat. The evangelist told this story reference to harvesting souls and that there was a major storm on the horizon and we needed to make hast to bring in the souls before it was too late.

I often wondered and wanted to ask to whose barn was the harvest gathered. Several combines worked together to save the harvest, but to whose barn was the harvest gathered? You see, too many preacher push for saving souls even if it means selfishly pulling sheep from another pastor's fold. I thoroughly appreciate visiting preachers like Joyce Meyers or Benny Hinn who take the time to find out the churches in the areas where they preach and then refer the souls that come up for salvation to churches that they can attend in their area. Let's face it: there are no big I's and little yous in God's kingdom. No man has all of the answers. There are those that have a little more light in some areas that others; however, the mistake is to think that one has so much light that all must come to him and him alone. Preachers who think like this do not offer anything to a struggling ministry. I have even heard one pastor suggest to another to come give up what he was doing for God, bring all of his few people, and sit under that pastor's ministry. But the word of God says look to another man's wealth and not just your own. So why not give to that pastor's small and struggling ministry whatever it needs to grow and become a strong thriving ministry instead of taking from it to build your own? There are enough people needing to be saved to fill every church in America ten times over. Love at work in the heart of every member of the body of Christ would look to another man's things and seek to get people saved and to the place where God would have them to be instead of just trying to increase their own numbers. Telling a person to leave the state that they are in just to come to your church without God specifically ordering such a move is not love.

No, love is not selfish. Love looks not just to its own things but also the things of others. Another way that this occurs is in a situation that I encountered on one of my previous jobs. I was working in accounting and needed to collect some money on an account. I was making calls to the responsible family member and ended up in a forty-five-minute conversation with a woman who was blind and her husband was crippled. This couple used to attend my church. She said there were several different lay leaders who took up the task of picking her and her husband up to bring them to church. Each one would pray with them, lay hands on them, and encourage them to believe for their healing. But when they did not receive their healing in that lay leader's time, they each dropped off picking the couple up to bring them to church. The woman said that she felt like each lay leader was seeking the glory of being the one to get this couple healed. When it did not happen, the lay leaders stopped trying and stopped picking them up for church. The Amplified version of 1 Corinthians 13:5 says love does not insist on its own right or its own way, for it is not self-seeking. If the lay leaders were not self-seeking, they would have continued to pick this couple up for church and let God move on them in His time and His way. So that if the woman never received her sight and the man never walked again, they would not have had to change where they worshipped to find people who would get them to church. Being generous does not mean we are not selfish, and love, God's love in us is not selfish.

9

Love Is Not Easily Provoked

*Charity suffereth long, and is kind; charity envieth not; charity
vaunteth not itself, is not puffed up, Doth not behave itself
unseemly, seeketh not her own, is not easily provoked.*

—1 Corinthians 13:4–5

*Love endures long and is patient and kind; love never is envious
nor boils over with jealousy, is not boastful or vainglorious, does not
display itself haughtily. It is not conceited (arrogant and inflated with
pride); it is not rude (unmannerly) and does not act unbecomingly.
Love (God's love in us) does not insist on its own rights or its own
way, for it is not self-seeking; it is not touchy or fretful or resentful.*

—Amplified Version, Classic Edition

Every one of these eight things that love does not do is an area for
growth in all men. However, there are certain ones that deserve extra
attention, and I believe this is one of them. I included the Amplified
version of this scripture to bring special attention to what Apostle Paul
was saying when he said love is not easily provoked. If you are like me,
when I first read this part about love, I thought I was hitting it if I did
not get angry about something very easily. I thought if I held my peace
and did not get upset and fly off of the handle, then I had arrived.

As a child growing up, I live most of my childhood years living with my mother's boyfriend who is the father of the four youngest children in my family. He was not a pleasant person to live with and always liked to provoke my father's children to be disrespectful so that he would have a reason to beat on us. He would have a field day with certain of my siblings, but when he came to try to provoke me, I would hear the still small voice of the Holy Spirit say, "Don't say nothing." So I would not say anything. In fact, hearing the Holy Spirit speak to me would give me the strength and courage to look him straight in the eye and not say a word. When I did not talk back to my mother's boyfriend, he had to turn and go away from me because he did not get what he was looking for to start a fight. When I saw the results of not allowing him to provoke me, I tried to teach it to my siblings older than me, but they would never listen. When he would come to them to provoke them to anger and start a fight with them, he got just what he wanted because they did not keep quiet and talked back to him and gave him the provocation that he needed to justify a fight with them.

Now as an adult, I find myself striving to get back to that place and suffering through situations that I have no business having to endure because I lost that ability to resist being provoked. I wondered why I could not resist and look temptation in the eye but still hold my peace. I found out my love had grown cold in this area. I had gotten to be a legal adult, and thought I could stand up for myself. The moment I turned eighteen, I thought, *I can speak for myself now. I can stand up for myself now. Anybody messing with me had better be ready for a fight now 'cause I ain't gotta take no stuff off nobody now.* Little did I know that I had a lot to learn. Just because we become adults does not mean that we will never need to exercise self-control. Pastor Creflo Dollar has a teaching series on controlling your emotions that would benefit every man greatly. All these many years and situation after situation on the job, in the classroom, and even in the church, I have finally come to the realization that walking in love toward others include not allowing myself to be provoked to anger by any situation and act in ways that does not represent Christ.

One of the ways that God helped me in this area is through a teaching session with Gloria Copeland and Billy Brim. I love to watch Christian television, and "Kenneth Copeland Ministries" is one of my favorites. This day Gloria Copeland had Billy Brim on as a guest, and Billy was giving her testimony about how God had dealt with her about her attitude toward her husband. Just like me, Billy had been meditating on the second part of the Amplified version of 1 Corinthians 13:5 where it says that love takes no account of a thing done to it, pays no attention to a suffered wrong. I had meditated it, mutter it, recited it, and everything else you could do with it. But I was still missing the mark most of the time. Well, I just kept on meditating, muttering, and reciting figuring I would eventually get to where I was actually doing it. Meanwhile, I was always acting like I had to defend myself and speak up for myself which often brought me misery. Finally I started praying to God about that area of my life. I observed my own situation and those around me, especially in the church. I have watched people come and go because they were provoked to anger about a situation. If God tells you to go to a certain church, why would you allow things that you encounter in that church to cause you to leave the place where God told you to go? That is my question to anyone who says God told me to do this or that. If God said it, that should settle it, and no matter what we encounter, we should remain fixed on what God said. God is love. I cannot say that enough. He has poured His love into all of us who has received Jesus Christ as Lord and Savior of our lives. He has poured His love upon all men because He sent Jesus to die *for all men* and provided a way to escape the wrath to come. It is up to each one of us to appropriate God's love for us individually.

Therefore, in my quest to get to a point where I was not allowing myself to be provoked and stirred to anger, God used Billy Brim to bring the first part of the Amplified verse to my attention. Love is not touchy, fretful, or resent. Now that is a word. It lit up in my spirit like a 150-watt bulb. You see, most of us do not think of love in that likeness. Somehow, we miss the connection between not being touchy, fretful, or resentful and remaining calm and self-controlled when we encounter situations that either threaten us or simply fail to give us our way. What about you? Are you touchy, fretful, or resentful toward any person or any situation pressing you right now? Is this a place for you to grow in your love walk?

> *For even hereunto were ye called: because Christ also suffered for us, leaving us an example, that ye should follow His steps: Who did no sin, neither was guile found in His mouth: Who, when He was reviled, reviled not again; when He suffered, He threatened not; but committed Himself to Him that judgeth righteously:* (1 Pet. 2:21–23)

Love is not easily provoked or stirred to anger. There is no better example than that which Christ laid for us to follow in terms of anger control. He is our perfect example, and He would not require us to do something that He has not equipped us to do. In all of the gospels' depictions of His life, there is only one mention of Jesus displaying anger, and that was righteous anger over the misuse of the house of God. But He showed us an even greater way by the stories of His daily custom. He spent His days moving amongst the people. The scripture says He went about doing good and healing all that was oppressed of the devil. During His travels, He consistently encountered Pharisees and Sadducees who attempted to provoke Him with every manner of question and accusation. Jesus was called gluttonous and a wine bibber because He chose to eat and fellowship with those that needed Him the most. He was asked all kinds of question in an attempt to provoke Him or find an excuse to accuse Him wrongfully. But never once did Jesus get upset or show frustration. Instead He responded with calm words of wisdom that literally shut down His enemies. The peace that He had is what He gives to all who calls upon Him, and He expects us to walk in it. Doing so will not only improve our own lives daily but also demonstrate His goodness to others and draw them to repentance.

10

Love Does Not Think Evil

*Charity suffereth long, and is kind; charity envieth not; charity
vaunteth not itself, is not puffed up, Doth not behave itself unseemly,
seeketh not her own, is not easily provoked, thinketh no evil.*

—1 Corinthians 13:4–5

Love does not take inventory in evil, estimate evil, impute evil, recon
or suppose or account or deliberate to do evil. It is amazing the understanding we receive when we take time to look up the Greek words
translated into English. My initial thought about love not thinking
evil was that I was to not think about doing evil to anybody. But this
verse of scripture has a deeper meaning to it than that, and if we tap
into that deeper meaning and practice it, it will bring a great harvest
to our life. Make no mistake about it, practicing is not going to be
easy. But it is doable by the help of the Holy Ghost. The Amplified
version helps to bring out the deeper meaning of this portion of verse
5. It says, "It takes no account of the evil done to it [it pays no attention to a suffered wrong]." Now this is where faith has to come in.
Because I don't know about you, but some of the wrongs that I have
suffered have made me want to check and see if that body had a heart
in it at all. I am not just talking about Christian folk either, so don't
get stuck on looking at people in the church. People—period—Black
and White, foreign and American has made me wonder if they have

a conscience at all. We tend to focus on the church and Christians, yet there are those that do not go to church but consider themselves morally good and philanthropic toward people who say or do things that make you wonder what side of Mars they came from.

For example, this thing about partial birth abortion would not be an issue if we all were walking in line with the things that love does or does not do as outlined in the pages of this book. To call and unborn child a thing and calculate how much money can be made by selling its parts to research companies; then go about killing them by birthing everything but the head just to stick scissors into the back of the skull to make a hole to suck out it brains is downright beastly. Love, God's love in us could not, would not think that kind of evil toward any live creature. If it has a heart that beats, it is a living creature. Isn't it amazing that the very people that would perform partial birth abortion on an unborn child would not think of doing that to their dog.

Another way that love does not think evil is by lying on a person or bearing false witness against a person. Jesus suffered this continually throughout His ministry to the very people that ended up accusing Him and causing Him to be crucified. He was accused of being a wine bibber because he sat and ate with sinners. He was accused of being a devil because He was casting devils out of people and healing them. So I reckon that if Jesus could go about doing good and healing all who were oppressed of the devil and still be lied on and falsely accused, then the same can be done to anybody. That is not an act of love, and all of us who profess Jesus Christ as Lord and Savior of our lives should be examples of Him and do what He does.

Another way to look at this is love takes no account of the thing done to it and pays no attention to a suffered wrong so that it does not think about evil ways to get back at a person for the wrong incurred. I am sure that we can all think about things that we have suffered, especially the extremely hurtful things, and consider the thoughts we had about how to get back at the person who caused the hurt. I remember when I first moved to Columbus, Ohio, and some things that were done to my family and me while we were trying to get adapted and established in our new environment. I spent the first two years praying for two separate families who somehow thought they had a right to feed off us and falsely accuse us and me in particular because I was the head of my family and the vessel God used to stabilize us in our new location. During those two years, I prayed constantly, not just for the two families but for myself also. You see, I had all kinds of thoughts about what I should do to combat against the abuse and false accusation that I suffered. However, the love of God always prevailed in me simply because of my prayers for the two families and my willingness to submit to the word of God rather than the thoughts that came to my mind concerning things I could do to or about those two families. When I got to the point that I would not ponder the thoughts but resist them, then God stepped in and dealt with those families His way.

11

Love Does Not Rejoice in Iniquity

Charity suffereth long, and is kind; charity envieth not; charity vaunteth not itself, is not puffed up, Doth not behave itself unseemly, seeketh not her own, is not easily provoked, thinketh no evil; rejoiceth not in iniquity.

—1 Corinthians 13:4–6

Rejoiceth—(5463) *Chairo /khah'-ee-ro/*, to be cheerful, i.e., calmly happy or well off; imper. espec. as salutation (on meeting or parting), be well, be glad, God speed, greeting, joy (fully).

This passage of scripture is an example of two different Greek words translated to the same English word; however, the Greek meaning of the word is similar yet different. The Greek word translated *rejoiceth* in reference to iniquity is a prime root word from which other words are derived, but the prime word has a somewhat different meaning from the word derived from it. The Greek word in rejoiceth not in iniquity means to be cheerful and calmly happy on the inside. It means to be well, glad, or joyful on the inside when we see iniquity happening around us. It refers to the person who would see their brother falling into the sin of adultery, fornication, drugs and alcohol, or financial fraud or the likes thereof and pretends to be sympathetic about it on the outside while calmly rejoicing on the inside because that brother or sister has fallen. We see this characteristic in all people and on every level both Christian and secular. But it is most prominent among leaders and prevalent in the church. I have not seen as much gossiping and backbiting in the church as I have in the past two decades. Divorce between pastors and church leaders is more prominent now, and so is the gossip and finger-pointing. I pray for all pastors and church leaders and give thanks for them all whether God has appointed them or not because God is the final deciding factor in every ministry.

I remember how God had to correct me concerning one of my previous pastors by speaking to me through Pastor John Osteen referencing how God feels concerning His servants. God asked me this question:

> *Who art thou that judgest another man's servant? To his own master he standeth or falleth. Yea, he shall be holden up: for God is able to make him stand.* (Rom. 14:4)

> *Who are you to pass judgment on and censure another's household servant? It is before his own master that he stands or falls. And he shall stand and be upheld, for the Master (the Lord) is mighty to support him and make him stand.* (AMPC)

All men are born with the innate propensity to sin. Being born again does not mean that we will not sin. It simply means we will not deliberately practice sin. Likewise, being in leadership position does not mean that people cease to be human and lose the propensity to sin. It simply means that we lose the desire to sin and rejoice in it.

Far too many times I have observed leaders get in the pulpit and preach about the sins of other leaders and do so with joy. Politicians get on TV and verbalize the sins of other politicians, but no one ever seem to take into account what God has to say about that other person's sins or whether or not that other person has repented before God about the sins that they committed. I personally know the sting of negative words spoken out of joyful spite about my past sin. Those people who spoke about me never took into account the sins that were in their own life. They never consider the possibility that maybe I have gone to God and repented of that sin and was brought back into right fellowship with Him. So who are you, brother man, who pass judgment on another man's servant? And what about Galatians 6:1 which tells us that if any man is taken in a fault, those of us who are spiritual should restore that person with a spirit of meekness while considering ourselves lest we also be tempted. Oh no, you might not be tempted to commit adultery, at least not outwardly. But my Bible says whoever looks on a woman to lust after her commits adultery in his heart. I know we forgot about that scripture, but it is still there. I am well inclined to agree with Brother Kenneth E. Hagin who often emphasized the fact that the problem is that few of us are spiritual. I wish to God that others would pray and have often wanted to cry out from the pews and say let's pray for them right now. What if the whole Christian nation had fallen on their knees and prayed for President Bill Clinton when he sinned with Monica Lewinsky? What do you think would have happened if the whole body of Christ would have fallen on our knees and prayed for Randy and Paula White, Bishop Weeks and Prophetess Juanita Bynum-Weeks, Bishop Clarence McClendon, and others like them that have succumbed to the lust of their flesh or emotions? Instead there is more of that inner joy or gladness that a brother or sister has fallen. But love does not rejoice in iniquity, anyone's iniquity.

The scripture says consider yourself lest you also be tempted, but it does not say that we will be tempted the same way. No, the devil will not tempt me the same way that he may tempt you. I may not be susceptible to the same thing that you are susceptible to. But that does not mean that I am not susceptible to something, and I know that I had better be careful that I do not judge others and calmly delight in their troubles because trouble can come to me and catch me in my weaknesses just like it caught you.

> *I exhort therefore, that, first of all, supplications, prayers, intercessions, and giving of thanks, be made for all men; for kings, and for all that are*

in authority; that we may lead a quiet and peace-
able life in all godliness and honesty. For this is good
and acceptable in the sight of God our Savior; Who
will have all men to be saved, and to come unto the
knowledge of the truth. (1 Tim. 2:1–3)

This is a very key scripture for our nation and for the world. We are to pray for all men no matter who they are and especially for those in positions of authority in the world and in the church. If we are praying like the scripture encourages us to do, we would not rejoice in any man's iniquity, but we would earnestly pray for them with great hope that they would come to the knowledge of the truth of the word of God as it relates to that sin.

The Greek word translated *iniquity* actually means injustice. It denotes wrongfulness of character life or act and represents unrighteousness. I first became aware of the magnitude of this word while I was a member of the first Pentecostal church that I attended. In this Pentecostal organization, all the churches had clubs. There was the new member's club, youth department, willing workers club, and the missionary department. Every "good" member belonged in a club. I spent two years in the new member's club to make special people happy before I was finally released to the youth department. The craziness of all of this is that people of all ages were place into both clubs.

If you were under thirty-five, you were a member of the new member's club or a member of the youth department. This leaves the question, when do people grow up and start behaving as adults? The biblical teaching in this church was so weak, and government was so lax that it meant nothing to spend Saturday night partying, reveling, and fornicating and get up on Sunday morning and sing on the choir, dance, shout yourself snotty, and call yourself worshipping God.

One of these occasions we were having one of our youth department meetings, and the president of the youth department began to make fun of two of the ladies of the youth department who had decided to put on booty shorts and go to a popular park hunting down men. Those ladies were out all night the past Saturday night and leading choir songs on Sunday morning, and the youth department president thought this was something to laugh about and make fun of it.

After this meeting, the very next time I was reading my Bible, the Lord showed me the true, or should I say total, meaning of this scripture. You see, most of us read 1 Corinthians 13:6 and think this scripture is saying that a person that is walking in love does not rejoice in the evil that they do. But there are two sides to this scripture. Not only do we not rejoice in the evil that we do, but we also do not rejoice in the evil that others do. We should never make fun of or be happy about another person's sin. In fact, Ephesians 5:12 tells us that it is a shame to even speak of those things done in darkness. We are not to fellowship in it by talking about it and making fun of the act or the person. We are to expose it. But we are not to expose it by setting with others and gossiping about it.

Love does not rejoice in iniquity. Love is never calmly happy, cheerful, and joyful about the sin committed by any man, especially one that is of the household of God. We should not rejoice in the sins that we commit or the sins committed by others. Love covers a multitude of sin, and if we do speak of it, it should be to that brother or sister who sinned in an effort to minister to them and bring them to repentance. I am still waiting for those who backbite, gossip about, and belittle me to come and attempt to minister to me just once. I will gladly receive you even if your heart is not sincere because at least you came.

12

Love Rejoices in the Truth

Charity suffereth long, and is kind; charity envieth not; charity
vaunteth not itself, is not puffed up, Doth not behave itself
unseemly, seeketh not her own, is not easily provoked, thinketh
no evil; rejoiceth not in iniquity, but rejoiceth in the truth.

1 Corinthians 13:4–6

Truth (225)—*aletheia /al-ay'-thi-a/*, truth, truly as a noun used (1) objectively, (1a) signifying the reality lying at the basis of an appearance; the manifested, veritable essence of a matter, (1b) especially of Christian doctrine: where the truth of the gospel denotes the "true" teaching of the gospel, in contrast to the perversion of it.

Rejoiceth (4796)—*sugchairo /soong-khah'-ee-ro/*, from 4862 and 5463, to sympathize in gladness, congratulate: rejoice in (with).

Now we get back to the things that love does. We started out with the first two things that love does because we need to understand the initial characteristics of love. Love suffers long and is patient and kind or remains serviceable and employable. Even if we never take advantage of the provisions that God made for us through His Son, Jesus Christ, God still loves us, and He continues to suffer long and remains open to be serviceable and employable to us no matter what we do while we are on this earth. He is always wide open and waiting for us to repent of our sins and turn to Him. Does this mean that

He is not a just and righteous God? No, it just means that He is ever ready to receive us when we turn from our wicked way and determine to appropriate the salvation that he afforded us through the blood of His Son while we are on this earth.

Then we take a sidestep into the things that love does not do. After learning the things that love does not do and setting our heart to act on what we have learned, then we come to the rest of the things that love does. The first of the last six things deals with how we rejoice. Remember I told you the verse in 1 Corinthians 13:6 contains two different words translated rejoiceth. There is the prime Greek word that deals with rejoice as it relates to iniquity and a derivative word that deals with rejoice as it relates to truth. The word that is translated rejoiceth as it relates to truth is *sugchairo*, and it means to sympathize in gladness, congratulate, rejoice in or with. This is supposed to be what we do when we see other people being blessed and receiving good things in their life. By all means don't ask a sister how she gets to have a house better than yours. I once had an associate visit me when I lived in a three-bedroom house that had one-and-a-half-bath bathroom, a private bricked-in patio, and a car port. She really thought this house was something and was so jealous that she had to rephrase her words three times to ask me how I managed to find this house. "How you get to uh, uh… I mean why you get to uh, uh…" Can you just be happy for me and rejoice with me that God saw fit to bless me in this manner? The truth is I am blessed, and love rejoices in the truth.

The Amplified version of verse 6 says love rejoices when right and truth prevail. Breaking down the word *sympathize*, we see that *sym* means same and *path* means feel. So we are to rejoice with others and have the same glad feelings with others when righteousness and truth prevails. We are to congratulate it, rejoice in it and with it. I was watching an usher in my church rejoicing over a woman's testimony where she had been on drugs, gone to jail, and, while in jail, received books and tape messages that my pastor had preached. The woman was so moved by the messages that when she got out of jail, she visited my church, received salvation, and ended up attending Bible college fully paid by someone she did not know. That woman had so much joy over her new life that she jumped and shouted, and the usher jumped and shouted with her, feeling what she felt and sympathizing in gladness with her. We should not have to know a person to sympathize in gladness with them. That should be a natural flow of love.

Love rejoices in the truth. The other part to this is understanding what truth this verse is referring to. The word translate truth is *aletheia* and signifies the reality lying at the basis of an appearance, the manifested, veritable, genuine, authentic, or real essence of a matter. This definition reminds me of many situations that I have seen and most Christians know well. There is always more to any given circumstance than what lies at the surface. Love will always look deeper seeking to know the core or basis of a matter.

For years I have been accused of being a lesbian. That is far from the truth, and I have always tried to show others, prove to others that is far from the truth. Let me emphasize right here that I do not hate homosexuals. I am not opposed to homosexuality; I am opposed to sin and perversion. I believe in all of the word of God, and that includes what He says concerning homosexuality. My truest friend was a homosexual guy named Doug, and he was far more of a friend to me than I was to him. However, one day I started to take a closer look at when was the first time anyone ever accused me of homosexuality. As I thought about it, I realized that my current location is not the first place where I was accused and that the first accusation goes all the way back to when I was eleven years old. Society has come a long way from where we used to be when I was a child. I grew up in a hush-hush generation where children were made to be seen and not heard, and the part of the body above the knees and below the waist was never discussed. The male and female organs, their purpose and functionality were never a topic of any discussion. So when I had my first menstrual cycle, I only knew what to do because of what I saw happening around me and the errands I had to run going to the store to make purchases for my mother and oldest sister. When it became my turn, I made a point of reading and researching everything that could be known about the process starting with the information on the sanitary napkin box. Any word that I did not understand I made a note of and used the next school library trip to further my research. I found out where babies came from and, at the tender age of eleven, decided that I was not going to be like my mother bearing a bunch of kids that I could not afford and blaming them for their life. I determined in my heart that I would not have sex until I graduated from high school. I was very neglected as a child, and when my clothes wore out, I did not get replacements right away. This meant having to wear some of my brothers' clothes. My hair had been cut and was not very well kept, so I wore an afro before it became popular in the late '60s to do so.

So because of my determination not to have sex at a young age, the devil used the boys that were after me to accuse me of being homosexual. Because I did not want to have sex, had to wear my brothers' clothes, and wore a short bush hairstyle, I must be gay, only back then they called lesbians dykes and bull daggers. That was the superficial appearance the devil used to belittle me and steal some of my self-esteem. That is the purpose of all accusation, to steal confidence and self-esteem from a person to bring them down to a position of compromise and submission. The truth is always visible if we look for it, and love would always love for the truth and rejoice in it when it is found.

> *But the Lord said unto Samuel, look not on his countenance, or on the height of his stature; because I have refused him: for the Lord seeth not as man seeth; for man looketh on the outward appearance, the Lord looketh on the heart.* (1 Sam. 16:7)

God looks at every man's heart. He sees beyond the surface, deep into the soul of every man. He knows the thing that we all encounter in life that try to derail us from His purpose for our lives. There is not a rape or beating or an abuse of any kind, emotional or physical, that God do not know about. There is not even a secret thought that escapes Him. Yet He is always ready to entreat us when we turn to Him. Jesus died for the sins of man so that there could be more of Him in the earth. God pours out His spirit into the hearts of all who come to Him so that we can be like Him to show others the love that looks beyond the surface of a matter, beyond the countenance of any person to see the inner truth, the hidden man of the heart. The truth is there is not a single human being on the face of this earth that is perfectly holy and without sin. We all need a savior. We all need somebody to look past our outer appears to see our heart. Find the most evil and hard person on earth today and examine his or her life and you will find that there was a time, thing, or situation that brought that person to where they are; and if that truth about that person had been discovered at the beginning, that person would be in a different place today.

Love rejoices in the truth. Not just the truth as man sees it because man's vision is limited. Love rejoices in the truth of God's word and the reality of it applied to the circumstances of life here on earth. So when we hear of a ministry gift failing and succumbing to some sort of sin, we rejoice when truth and righteousness prevail in that situation. We pray for them. I'll say that again. We pray for them and entreat God's mercy for and upon them and expect God's intervention for them that they will recover. Love sympathizes gladly in the reality lying at the basis of an appearance, the manifested, veritable, genuine, authentic, or real essence of a matter because that is where the truth lies.

13

Love Bears All Things

Charity suffereth long, and is kind; charity envieth not; charity vaunteth not itself, is not puffed up, Doth not behave itself unseemly, seeketh not her own, is not easily provoked, thinketh no evil; rejoiceth not in iniquity, but rejoiceth in the truth; beareth all things.

—1 Corinthians 13:4–7

Bear ye on another's burdens, and so fulfill the law of Christ.

—Galatians 6:2

Love bears up under anything and everything that comes.

1 Corinthians 13:7

Bear means everything you think it means, but we must dig deeper to fully understand how love bears all things. There are six different Greek words translated *beareth* in the New Testament. Only one refers to bearing all things as it relates to love. The word translated *beareth* in 1 Corinthians is *stego* and actually means to roof over, to cover with silence and patiently endure. If every member of the body of Christ spent one hour a day practicing this attribute of love, gossip would take a serious nosedive, criticism would become tongue-tied, and every other act that would injure a brother or sister would cease for that one hour. This is exactly what Peter said in 1 Peter 4:8 when he said to above all things have fervent love among us because love will cover the multitude of sin.

Does this mean we are to turn our backs and ignore sin amongst us? Absolutely not, preachers should preach the word of God; teachers should teach the word of God and then love all people while they grow spiritually in spite of the wrong things they do during the growing process. Then after a period of time when baby Christians should have grown up and put on Christ, if they continue to wallow in sin, we ought to do what Paul described in 1 Corinthians 5 and separate ourselves from fellowship with that person. However, what I am learning about all of this is to stop complaining and telling anybody about the situations that I encounter in interpersonal relationships. One of my greatest lessons was at my previous church. I spent ten years praying, crying sometimes, arguing, and almost fighting. Every Sunday service, Wednesday night Bible study, and almost every other fellowship was an adventure. One time my pastor made me so angry I told God I wanted to hit him. I told God I wanted to burst his lip, but no, that would heal to fast. I wanted to punch him in the nose, but no, that would disappear as soon as it stopped bleeding. Then I thought I wanted to blacken his eye by hitting him on the bridge of the nose just like my brother hit my sister. But no, that wouldn't last long enough either. Finally I thought, I wanted to put on a boxing glove, catch him unawares, and hit him with a right cross near the end of his chin and break his jaw. Then he would have had to have his jaw wired shut to heal. He would have to talk and preach through wired jaws, and everyone would want to know what happened to him. The whole time I was talking to God and saying all of this, the Holy Spirit was saying to me, "Touch not my anointed and do my Prophet no harm." I asked God, "Am I not also your anointed?" Nevertheless, this was one of those times that I had to exercise love that covers with silence and endures patiently. It was not easy, and I almost got in trouble with God again about my attitude toward His people and the things that I was experiencing. But God loves all His creation no matter what. He also corrects His children the way that

He sees fit, and He is the only one that can bring righteous correction to any man.

This is where Galatians 6:2 comes in. The word here is *bear* and represents what we do at a given moment. The word is *bastazo*, and it means to lift, literally or figuratively, to endure, declare, sustain, carry, and take up. So what I had to do for that pastor was to lift him up to God in prayer for, and I must emphasize for him. I had to endure the situation and declare God's word over him, the situation, and me. I had to sustain my position as a member of that church and continue to pay tithes and offerings and do those things that were pleasing in God's sight and let God deal with my pastor as He saw fit. We must remember that God is love, and what He is we are because we are made in His image. That being the case, it is required of us to show His love in the midst of every situation that we encounter. We cannot do this if we do not know Him and are not familiar with His attributes of love. That is the purpose of this writing. We must come to fully understand the attributes of love if we are to win people to Christ and bear fruit that remains before He returns to rapture His body.

I am fully persuaded that this is the last wave of the move of God in the earth restoring to the church the things it had lost. First, it was the return to righteousness by faith through Martin Luther, then sanctification through John Wesley. Then in the twentieth century, the church experienced the return of the Holy Spirit with the evidence of speaking in tongues, then divine healing, then the word of faith and gifts of the Holy Spirit and prosperity. God does not want His people poor. If He did, He would not give us the power to get wealth (Deut. 8:18). These were all waves of the move of God on the church, and I believe this last wave is the return of the God kind of love to those that are His people to draw all people, as many that will come to Him in these last days before the door is closed where no man can come.

14

Love Believes All Things

*Charity suffereth long, and is kind; charity envieth not;
charity vaunteth not itself, is not puffed up, Doth not behave
itself unseemly, seeketh not her own, is not easily provoked,
thinketh no evil; rejoiceth not in iniquity, but rejoiceth
in the truth; beareth all things; believeth all things.*

1 Corinthians 13:4–7

Love is ever ready to believe the best of every person.

—Amplified Version

Now this is one of my areas of sensitivity, you might say. Joyce Meyer coined the phrase "hurting people hurt people." I could add on to that, "hurting people don't trust." You might ask, "Don't trust what or don't trust who?" To which I would respond, anything or anybody? You see, people who have been hurt like I have been hurt do not want to open themselves up for that kind of hurt again. So we put up those walls that say no, don't let them in and don't believe nothing they say. If they say the color is blue, make them prove it. My daughter once quoted the Amplified version on verse 7 to me, and I tried to make and argument out of the two words *ever ready.*

My position was I am ever ready to believe the best, but I am always on the lookout.

Now I like to always give the Greek meaning of a word since the New Testament was originally written in Greek and translated into English. The Greek word for *believeth* is *pisteuo* and is pronounced *pist-yoo'-o*, and it means to have faith in, upon or with respect to a person or thing. It means to entrust, believe, commit, put in trust with. Some people gain financial wealth and set up trust funds for their children and grandchildren. That means they put money in the hands of a bank or financial institution that will be available for their children and grandchildren for a future time while it makes money and grow; they are waiting for that time to come. Just like putting money in the bank expecting to come back and get when we want to, we are to ready to put our trust in every person expecting to receive good from them. That does not mean that we are to open ourselves up to dishonesty and deception. God has given us wisdom and the ability to discern, and He expects us to use what He has given us. We should pay attention to, follow that inward witness that warns us of danger, and harm before it reaches us. But we should not go around being suspicious of everything and everybody we encounter. Suspicious people are fearful people. God has not given us a spirit of fear. Fear is of the devil, it brings torment, and its purpose is to rob us of the good things that God has for us.

One of the hardest lessons that I have had to learn and greatest adjustments that I have had to make is learning to open up my own heart and learn to have faith in people even when they make mistakes. I have made plenty of mistakes and lost some good friends because of it. The word of God is true and works for anyone who acts on it, and God's word says we reap what we sow (Gal. 6:7). I need to be forgiven sometimes. I need for people to have faith in me, entrust themselves to me, and know that I have their best interest in mind. Since I have that need, I ought to be sowing and always ready to sow faith and trust in others.

15

Love Hopes All Things

Charity suffereth long, and is kind; charity envieth not; charity vaunteth not itself, is not puffed up, Doth not behave itself unseemly, seeketh not her own, is not easily provoked, thinketh no evil; rejoiceth not in iniquity, but rejoiceth in the truth: beareth all things, believeth all things, hopeth all things.

—1 Corinthians 13:4–7

Its hopes are fadeless under all circumstances.

—Amplified Version

This is one of the most difficult things for those who are enduring great hardship or the prolonged fulfillment of desires to do. Abraham waited for twenty-five years for the fulfillment of God's promise of a seed. Abraham received the promise of a son, but even his faith got weak and settled for Ishmael. After waiting ten years, it did not take much for Sarah to talk him into using her maid to obtain a child. Sarah laughed at the prospect, but Abraham fell on his face and laughed. But God proved Himself faithful to all of His promises to Abraham, and it is an example to us to encourage our hope. Love hopes all things and does not fade or weaken in any circumstance.

The love of God poured into all of us that are His causes us to keep hoping in the midst of the most detrimental circumstances.

The confident anticipation of the manifestation of future expectation is the best definition of hope. Without hope, our faith has nothing to work for. Without love, we do not hope for the difficult things. It is easy to hope for something that you know is going to happen at a set time. People who live in an all-weather climate but love the summer confidently anticipate the summer season on cold, icy winter days. Likewise, those who love the cold and snow look forward in anticipation when the summer temperatures reach ninety-eight degrees in the shade.

But what about that husband who is antagonistic and abusive who refuse to get counseling or do anything to amend his ways? Or what about that teenager that will not go to school but choose to hang out with others that have already dropped out? All your hopes for your child was that he or she would graduate from high school, go to college, and obtain that degree and professional career that has eluded your family for generations. Consider the young mother that has just been diagnosed with breast cancer whose mother also died from cancer, along with her grandmother who died from cancer. It is difficult to hope for good in such trying situations. Yet love hopes all things. The love of God in us causes us to hope for the seemingly hopeless situations.

The Greek word translated *hopeth* in 1 Corinthians 13:7 is *elpizo*, and it means to expect or confide, trust. It is derived from the prime word *elpis*, which means to anticipate, usually with pleasure; expectation or confidence. As I was reading this definition, I had to take special note of the word *confide*. I understand "to expect" because we all do that easily even when we should not. If you go to work for eight hours a day, I expect to receive a paycheck at the end of a week or two weeks. If you buy a house, you expect to pay a mortgage. However, what does it mean to confide?

The *Webster's Dictionary* definition of confide means "to tell or talk about as a secret: to entrust (as duty, object, person, etc. to someone); to give into the keeping of a trusted person." So that is what we do with our desires or the things that we hope for; we give it to the keeping of a trusted God that has never failed us ever and will never fail us. God is love. So we give our hopes, dreams, earnest desires, and most difficult situations into the keeping hands of the God who created us and predestined us to be where we are, doing what we are doing, no matter how difficult it is. God says He watches over His word to perform it, so we take Him at His word. The word of God tell us to pray in secrecy and He will reward us openly. Psalms 62:8 in the Amplified version says, *"Trust in, lean on, rely on, and have confidence in Him at all times, you people; pour out your hearts before Him. God is a refuge for us (a fortress and a high tower)."* I have had to do this many times in my life. I remember once when I was wrongfully fired from my good government job and had to live with my mother with my two daughters, one of which was a pregnant teenager. After a year and a half of living with people and struggling trying to prove my innocence and get my job back, I became so frustrated I sat on my mother's couch, raised my hands to God, and said, "God, if you don't help me, I am not going to make it." Suddenly, I felt like someone was pouring a think oil or ointment on the top of my head, and it slowly streamed down all over my body. The extreme anxiety that I had felt was replaced with warmth and peace that I cannot fully describe. In my despair, I confided in my God, my hope for restoration was renewed, and I was able to run on. My situation did not change for another year, but I was able to run on because my hope was renewed. My love for God enabled me to love those around me in the midst of my difficulties and continue to hope for the relief that I needed regardless to what the situation looked like. Love's hope in me was fadeless in spite of the hardship continuing and the people around me who were either totally insensitive and did not care or were overly sensitive and did not know God and therefore lacked the right words to encourage me on.

When the love of God is abiding in us, our hope is strengthened, and we are able to hope for the seemingly impossible. Cancer is healed because of this hope. Financial ruin is overturned by this hope. As we grow in this attribute of love, we will become mighty warriors of faith that cause the overturn of the devil's kingdom in many lives because our fadeless hope gives our faith work.

16

Love Endures All Things

Charity suffereth long, and is kind; charity envieth not; charity vaunteth not itself, is not puffed up, Doth not behave itself unseemly, seeketh not her own, is not easily provoked, thinketh no evil; rejoiceth not in iniquity, but rejoiceth in the truth: beareth all things, believeth all things, hopeth all things, endures all things.

—1 Corinthians 13:4–7

It endures everything [without weakening].

—Amplified Version

Endurance is the attribute of love that makes most of the body of Christ angry. I am talking about church hoppers, area hoppers (those that do not leave the church but move from one volunteer place to another frequently), and ministry hoppers. Too many people encounter hardship or become offended and take flight. They say, "God told me to come here." But the moment things do not go their way or the moment they disagree with something that is said or done, they take off. I am especially amazed with people like a man I met in 1998 who brought his wife and seven children to my present church saying that God told him to come here. He attended the new member's classes and introduced himself as Pastor So-and-so. He had other members of that class calling him pastor until I reminded them that there was only one pastor of this church. This brother tried his best to get on the leadership staff. When he realized that was not going to happen, he was gone in less than two years. Was that a representation of endurance?

The Greek work translated *endurance* is *hupomeno*. It is pronounced *hoop-om-en-o*, and it means to remain; figuratively it means to undergo or, in other words, to bear trials. It means to persevere, abide, take patiently, suffer, to have fortitude. Now there's a word for you. The *Webster's Dictionary* definition of *fortitude* is firm courage; patient endurance of misfortune, pain, etc. You tend to find this attribute in about a fourth of the members of any church. I was listening to one of my favorite television ministries who was teaching on church attendance. He stated how he wondered if he really had thirty thousand members based on the listed names of people that stated they were members of his church. He said as he reviewed attendance practices of the people he found that some only attended once or twice a month or only on Wednesday or maybe a few times a year such as special holidays. He is amongst many pastors I hear speak of watching people get up and walk out when he is preaching on areas of their sinfulness. We are all familiar with those who come based on what kind of music is playing or if there is any music at all. I have even had one of my family members tell she could not get into the previous church I attended because we had no music. She said she could not get into the service because we did not have good music and was not into all that teaching, so she stopped attending. That same family member was always calling on me to help her fight the devil.

Church attendance is greatly based on how people endure difficulties, and how well we endure difficulties is rooted in our love. The word *hupomeno* is derived from the primary verb *meno* which means to stay in a given place, state, relation, or expectancy. It further means to abide, continue, dwell, be present, remain, stand, and tarry for. All of this reminds me of how houses and apartments used to be built. When I was about eleven years old, my friends and I used to play in an apartment building while it was being built. I remember watching as they poured the cement and laid the foundation. Then they built up around the edges of the cement floor with cinder blocks. They did not stop the cinder blocks at ground level but continued up for two stories. Then they started from ground level and laid the brick and mortar outer shell of the building up the entire two stories. Only after the outer foundation was completed did they put in the wood flooring and woodwork for the inner walls. This was a building that was built to remain, and this is what love does during hard times. It remains; stays in place; and continues to abide, dwell, and be present in spite of the difficulty and hardship.

I had to learn how to remain and stand firmly courageous while patiently enduring the emotional pain of being falsely accused and treated like a wretch by all but three members of the church at every service I attended. As I said earlier, I dropped out of church at an early age and, as an adult, struggled to find a church I could call home. After being lead to my first Pentecostal church, I struggled through the first three years and was about to drop out because I felt I could no longer endure the pressure of trying to be a member of that church. But God, He always steps in right when we need Him most. Through acts of His will, I was strengthened, refreshed, and no longer desired to leave the place where He had sent me. Later on in that same church God spoke to me while I was at the altar praying and whining about something that someone had done to me, and He told me, "Stop whining, you whine too much. Endure hardship as a good soldier." Well, I remember reading that scripture in 2 Timothy 2:3: *"Thou therefore endure hardness, as a good soldier of Jesus Christ." The Amplified version says, "Take [with me] your share of the hardships and suffering [which you are called to endure] as a good (first-class) soldier of Christ Jesus."* This is what we are all called to do as children of the living God. Well, I stopped whining and set myself to endure whatever difficulties I encounter from that day forward. It has not been easy, but I love God, Jesus Christ, and His Holy Spirit; and with the help of the Trinity, I know I can overcome any difficulty, any hardship, and so can you.

Love endures everything without weakening. There would be no divorce, especially amongst Christians, if we all took the time to practice this attribute of love. God's love for mankind has endured thousands of centuries since Adam and Eve was created and placed in the garden of Eden.

> *The Lord hath appeared of old unto me, saying, Yea, I have loved thee with an everlasting love: therefore with lovingkindness have I drawn thee.*
> (Jer. 31:3)

God loves us. He loves all His creation even those that deny and disown Him. Because of His great love, He is patient and long-suffering, not willing that any man should perish but that all should come to the knowledge of truth and grace. Jesus wants to work through His body to show the love of God to those who do not know Him, but He cannot do that if we are not willing to *endure all things*.

17

Love Never Fails

Charity suffereth long, and is kind; charity envieth not; charity vaunteth not itself, is not puffed up, Doth not behave itself unseemly, seeketh not her own, is not easily provoked, thinketh no evil; rejoiceth not in iniquity, but rejoiceth in the truth: beareth all things, believeth all things, hopeth all things, endures all things. Charity never faileth.

—1 Corinthians 13:4–7

The Lord hath appeared of old unto me, saying, Yea,
I have loved thee with an everlasting love: therefore,
with loving kindness have I drawn thee.

—Jeremiah 31:3

God's love never ends. It never ceases to exist. This is a hard concept to grasp for some people. We ask, where was God when this tragedy hit or when a spouse walks away from a marriage where there was a previous confession on undying love? Where was God when my child died or when the fire burned up my home and all my earthly possessions? He was right there with you. He is always there waiting for us to turn to Him and receive the love He has for us that surpasses anything that we have ever known. The Greek word translated *faileth* actually means "to drop away; driven out of one's course; become inefficient; fall off or away, take none effect." In other words, God's love never drops away. In all the years of man, from Adam and Eve in the garden of Eden to this present day and time, our sinfulness has never driven God's love for us off course. It is still on course now in spite of the wretched condition of most of us.

God is sovereign, but He is not arbitrary. He is sovereign, but He does not force His will on anyone. He created man to be in fellowship with and to be an object of His love. In Him is no variableness nor shadow of turning (Jas. 1:17), so that will never change. But just because we reject Him does not mean His love ceases. Think about this: Paul was a murderer who hunted down Christians to kill or imprison them. Yet in the midst of a bounty hunting journey, God's love reached out to him so strongly that it knocked Paul off his horse and blinded him for three days to turn him from his course of destruction. That is exactly what God wants to do for all mankind, and He wants to do it through us who have received Him to others who need Him.

An excellent example of God's unfailing love, working through Christians, is in 1 and 2 Corinthians. Now check this out: this is a man who decided he had to have his father's wife. So not only was he a fornicator amongst tongue-talking Christians, but he also had to go the extreme as to do so with his stepmother (1 Cor. 5:1–13). Paul jumped in there, judged in the matter, turned the man over to Satan, and told the people of Corinth to put the man away from them and have nothing to do with him. There was a problem with part of that. But because of his separation from the people and the conviction of the Holy Spirit, the man repented of his sin and desired to be brought back into fellowship with the people of God. We know this because of what Paul says in 2 Corinthians 2:5–9. Paul encouraged the assembly at Corinth to forgive the man that had done the wrong and to confirm their love toward the man so that he would not be overcome by too much sorrow from being separated from them. This is truly an example of love that does not fail. Love does not stop loving because of sin. Love simply does not have any fellowship with sin. When a person persists in committing sin, those who are striving to live holy should not keep company with that person. However, if that person repents and turns away from that sin, we are to receive that person back into fellowship and confirm our love toward him/her, and that is what most members of the body of Christ fail to do. No, what too many encounter when they fall short and reveal their humanity is a bunch of gossiping, backbiting busybodies and judgers who truly either do not know the love of God or simply do not care to walk in it. Those who do not know God's love need to learn, and that is what this book is about. Those who do not care, this book is for you too because you are the main ones that are going to need it. Remember Galatians 6:7 which says, "Be not deceived: God is not mocked; for whatever a man soweth, that shall he also reap." We reap what we sow, and we all need love.

The problem with what Paul did in 1 Corinthians is that he judged and condemned the man to death. Now we are to judge whether a thing is right or wrong and then chose the right thing to keep our right standing with God. But no man has the right to condemn a man to death at this present time. There is coming a time when the righteous shall even judge angels, but that time is not yet and will not be until Jesus returns. No, Jesus demonstrated what we are to do as we follow in His steps by what He did when the people brought Him the woman who was caught in adultery. When the people pressed Jesus for and answer, as to whether they should follow the law of Moses or not, Jesus told them to let he who is without sin cast the first stone. Jesus's love for the woman did not fail. He was not driven off His course of love because of her sin. He loved her and refused to condemn her but spoke kind words to her telling her to go and sin no more, and she obeyed Him and became one of His staunch followers. As we follow in His steps, our love will not be driven off course of showing the love of God to others.

We should separate ourselves from those who practice sin. It is very true that bad company will spoil good morals. However, we are not to condemn anyone just as Jesus did not condemn anyone. If fact, He sat with them teaching them the word of God and showing them the goodness of God, and this brought them to repent of the sin in their life. God's love never fails for us, so it should never fail through us.

18

Putting It All Together

Things Love Does	Things Love Does Not Do
1. Love suffers long.	1. Love does not envy.
2. Love is kind.	2. Love does not vaunt itself.
3. Love rejoices in truth.	3. Love is not puffed up.
4. Love bears all things.	4. Love does not behave unseemly.
5. Love believes all things.	5. Love does not seek her own, is not selfish.
6. Love hopes all things.	6. Love in not easily provoked.
7. Love endures all things.	7. Love does not think evil.
8. Love never fails.	8. Love does not rejoice in iniquity.

Looking at the things love does and the things love does not do side by side, we see that there is an opposites relationship with each attribute that grows as it progresses. Love suffers long, but not if it is swollen with envy. Remember, for envy they gave Jesus over to be crucified. Arrogant people are never kind to anyone, sometimes not even themselves. People that are full of pride vehemently resist truth because truth would destroy the pedestal or throne where they often place themselves. If we find ourselves acting or responding in the negative attribute and look to the positive attribute, we see exactly what we need to do to bring ourselves over to the place God would have us to be. Compassion flows out of love. Health and healing is a result of love. It takes love to be able to put up with the unlovable. Peter asked Jesus, "How long will my brother offend me and I forgive him, until seven times?" But Jesus (Love) responded to Peter with the long-suffering and endurance of love and told him not until seven times but until seventy times seven in a day. Now you know that there is no human being alive today that is going to stay around a person that is offending them that many times in a day. If you are like me, you will go away and not come back around for a while, if at all. But God's mercies are new every morning (Lam. 3:23). Every morning we get a new start, a new chance to change, to be different, to be better.

A person who is full of hope because of the love that is in them will never be easily provoked to anger, to do wrong, or to lose faith in what they believe to receive from God. I have believed for some of my family members to receive the salvation that Christ died for them to receive, and it is only when my love started to grow cold that my hope weakened. I thank God for all the members of the fivefold ministry, my pastor and other pastors, and leaders and their television ministry that admonished, encouraged, and strengthened me to keep believing in spite of what I see or hear.

> *I therefore, the prisoner of the Lord, beseech you that you walk worthy of the vocation wherewith ye are called, with all lowliness and meekness, with long suffering, forbearing one another in love.* (Eph. 4:1–3)

The only way to forbear one another in love is to know the attributes of love and practice them every day with every person we meet, especially the unlovable because they are the ones who need it the most. Paul said I beseech you or I beg you; he was pleading with the people of Ephesus and all who reads this letter because he knew both the necessity and the blessing of the call to the love walk. He repeats this urgent request at the beginning of chapter 5.

> *Be ye therefore followers of God, as dear children; and walk in love, as Christ also hath loved*

us, and hath given himself for us an offering and a sacrifice to God for a sweetsmelling savour. (Eph. 5:1–2)

Followers of God act like Him. Unfortunately, far too many people call themselves Christians and have no resemblance of Christ. Jesus loved like the Father. He demonstrated that love by His compassion to every man. He sat with the publicans and sinners, but he did not become a publican or sinner. Instead He showed them love and compassion. He taught the people by His words and by His actions. He said any man who comes to Him, He would no wise cast out. He never judged any man, and He never condemned any man. It is the goodness of the Lord that leads to repenting, and He left us an example that we should follow in His steps.

19

Decision

I told you in chapter 1 that I would address the number nine later in the book, and I have reserved it for this final chapter, the decision. You see, we all make decisions every day, and those decisions are based on choices. We make the choice to get up out of bed every day. We make the choice to shower, get dressed, and go to work or not go to work. We make the decision to eat or not eat. Now we have another decision to make, and that is, what to do with the information enclosed in the contents of this book.

I call this decision rather than conclusion because of some wise counseling that I received years ago as a high school dropout being prepared for the next stage of my life. The psychologist assigned to counsel all of us who were forced to accept not being high school graduates did everything he could to give us other alternatives. After reviewing my overall situation, he asked me what I thought about my current state. When I said I had come to a conclusion, he encouraged me to change my attitude because conclusions are final. While I may have come to a conclusion, life itself had not concluded and would continue on pass my conclusion. So rather than come to a conclusion, I came to a decision because decisions can be changed whenever we see that it is not the right one for a given circumstance.

Now concerning the number nine, it is the number of judgment. I know that many would rather say that nine is the number of birthing and that children are born in nine months. However, that is not exactly true. The actual human gestation period is thirty-eight to forty-two weeks. The pregnancy cycle is counted from the beginning of the last menstrual period to the birth of the child which is forty weeks, or the time of conception which is approximately two weeks after the beginning of the last menstrual cycle to the birth of the child which is thirty-eight weeks. A child can be born up to two weeks early or at thirty-six weeks and still be considered normal. Anything short of thirty-six weeks is premature. A child can be born two weeks past forty weeks, which is still considered normal. Past forty weeks is overdue, and labor is usually induced.

Nine is the number of judgment or finality. All things pertaining to man culminates with the number nine. It is highly respected by those who study occult and mathematical sciences and considered to have powers not found in other numbers. For example, you can add the digits of the numbers that are multiples of nine and always get nine, i.e., $2 \times 9 = 18$ and $1 + 8 = 9$; $4 \times 9 = 36$ and $3 + 6 = 9$. I tried this with other numbers, and it does not work. I will not bore you with the detailed research invested in the number nine except to tell you that it is the number of finality and judgment. It is the number of my mother's last child before she was able to break away from the cruelty of my father.

I realize this is scary to some people. I know there was a time in my life where I would not have wanted to know this information because of the way I was living. We all remember the fear surrounding 1999 and the anticipation for what was going to happen when the year ended. So then we must ask ourselves, what does nine have to do with anything? Well, think about this: it is the number that follows the eight things. We may never get it completely right, but those of us who truly want to love and be loved enough to strive to practice the eight things that love does and resist doing the eight things love does not do will be blessed to be a blessing. Then, because we have judged ourselves and made the adjustments toward love that we needed to make, we will hear "very well, my good and faithful servant" rather than "depart from me, you worker of iniquity," and God's judgment will be to your favor rather than disfavor. In 1 Timothy 1:12, Paul wrote,

> *I give thanks to Him Who has granted me the*
> *[the needed] strength and made me able [for this],*
> *Christ Jesus our Lord, because He has judged and*
> *counted me faithful and trustworthy, appointing me*
> *to [this stewardship of] the ministry.* (AMPC)

However, those who chose to ignore these eight things and fail to walk in love as the scriptures has encourage us to do will be judged by God. John 15:2 tells us that every branch that bears no fruit He takes away. We must dwell in Christ to be like Him, and if we do not dwell in Him, we cannot be like Him. Those who do not dwell in Him will be thrown out like broken branches and wither; these branches are gathered together and burned in the fire.

Some people argue and rationalize about what fruit Jesus is talking about in this discourse. Some say that the fruit He is speaking of is new converts. But Jesus said, "As the Father has loved me, so have I loved you: continue in My love." He goes on to tell us that if we keep His commandment, we abide in His love, and His commandment is to love one another as He has loved us. Therefore, the fruit that Jesus is speaking of is love. If we fail to love one another, we fail to keep His commandment, in which case we fail to abide in Him and are cast out like broken-off branches and wither.

I urge you, make the decision to study these eight things on both sides and strive to put off the bad and put on the good. People should be drawn to church, not driven away. Remember Jeremiah 31:3 says, "With loving kindness He has drawn us." We are supposed to love not just in word but in deed and in truth, and the truth is we reap what we sow.

A word from God:

January 23, 2002

> *We are headed for a new time and a new era*
> *where the things of God are unimaginable. We will*

be doing things and moving in the realm of the spirit in a manner never previously known to man. A time when the unimaginable will be happening and the spirits of man will come to know God in a way that we have never known Him before. God will do through us, His people, things that He has never done before. So much so that people will literally be snatched out of the darkness that they are in. People will be translated in the spirit from place to place like no man has ever seen before. Tell that to the people and let them know that God will always be God if we let Him in our lives. No one can protect you like God. No one can deliver you like God. No one can cover and provide for you like God. The people need to know these things, and it is our responsibility as children of God to make them (the people) to know who God really is.

God loves all creation, it is His, and He loves all that He created, and He desires that none be lost, though some will because of their stubbornness. God's will is for none.

Greek Word Definitions

(All definitions are taken from *Strong's Exhaustive Concordance of the Bible*)

bear. (941) *bastazo* /*bas-tad'-zo*/—to lift, lit or fig (endure, declare, sustain, receive, etc.):—bear, carry, take up.

beareth. (4722) *stego* /*steg'-o*/—to cover with silence (endure patiently):—(for-) bear.

believe. (4100) *pisteuo* /*pist-yoo'-o*/—from 4102; to have faith (in, upon, or with respect to, a person or thing), i.e. credit; by impl. To entrust (espec. one's spiritual well-being to Christ):—believe (-r), commit (to trust), put in trust with.

    (4102) *pistis, pis'-tispersuasion*, i.e. credence; mor. conviction (of relig. truth, or the truthfulness of God or a relig. teacher), espec. reliance upon Christ for salvation; abstr. Constancy in such profession; by extension, the system of religious (Gospel) truth itself:-assurance, belief, believe, faith, fidelity.

endureth. (5278) *hupomeno* /*hoop-om-en'-o*/—to stay under (behind) i.e. remain fig. to undergo, i.e. bear (trials), have fortitude, persevere:-abide, endure, (take) patient (-ly), suffer, tarry behind.

envieth. (2206) *zeloo*—to have warmth of feeling for or against: zealously effect, desire, covet Gal. 4:17, 18 zealously affect, but not well.

faileth. (1601) *ekpipto /ek-pip'-to/*—from 1537 and 4098; to drop away; spec., to driven out on one's course: fig. to lose, become inefficient:—be cast, fail, fall (away, off), take none effect.

hopeth. (1679) *elpizo /el-pid-zo/*—from 1680 to expect or confide; trust (to anticipate, usually with pleasure); expectation, confidence:—faith, hope.

iniquity. (93) *adikia /ad-ee-kee'-ah/*—injustice (prop. the quality, by implication, the act); mor. Wrongfulness (of character, life or act): unrighteousness. Adikia denotes unrighteousness, literally unrighteous, a condition of not being right, whether with God, according to the standard of His holiness and righteousness, or with man, according to the standard of what man knows to be right by his conscience.

kind. (5541) *chresteuomai /khraste-yoo'-om-ahee/*—to show oneself useful, i.e. act benevolently:—be kind.

puffed. (5448) *phusioo /foo-see-o'-o/*—from 5449 in the primary sense of blowing; to inflate, i.e.(fig) make proud (haughty): puff up.

provoke. (3947) *paroxuno /par-ox-oo'-no/*—to sharpen alongside, to exasperate: easily provoked, stir, used metaphorically signifies to rouse to anger, was stirred in 1 Co. 13:5

rejoiceth. (4796) *sugchairo /soong-khah'-ee-ro/*—from 4862 and 54763, to sympathize in gladness, congratulate:—rejoice in (with) (the second rejoiceth in 1 Co. 13:6 in reference to rejoicing in the truth).

rejoiceth. (5463) *chairo /khah'-ee-ro/*—to be cheerful, i.e. calmly happy or well off; imper. espec. as salutation (on meeting or parting), be well, be glad, God speed, greeting, joy (fully) (the first rejoiceth in 1 Co. 13:6 in reference to rejoicing in iniquity).

seeketh. (2212) *zeteo* /*dzay-teh'-o*/—to see (lit or fig.) to worship (God) (in a bad sense) to plot (against life, go about, desire to seek how to do something, or what to obtain, to seek or strive after, to require or demand.

suffereth. (3114) *makrothumeo* /*mak-roth-oo-meh-o*/—to be long spirited; (obj.) forbearing or (sub) patient, have (long) patience, patiently endure.

thinketh. (3049) *logizomai* /*log-id-zom-ahee*/—to take inventory; estimate impute; recon, account; suppose; reason, to reckon whether b calculation or imputation, to deliberate and so to account; consider.

truth. (225) *aletheia* /*al-ay'-thi-a*/—truth, truly as a noun used (1) objectively, (1a) signifying the reality lying at the basis of an appearance; the manifested, veritable essence of a matter, (1b) especially of Christian doctrine: where the truth of the gospel denotes the "true" teaching of the gospel, in contrast to the perversion of it.

unseemly. (808) *aschemosune* /*as-kay-mos-oo'-nay*/—from 809; an indecency; by imp. The pudenda:—shame, that which is unseemly

vaunteth. (4068) *perpereuomai* /*per-per-yoo'-om-ahee*/—braggart; perh. By redupl. of the base of 4008; to boast; vaunt itself.

Bibliography

Bullinger, E. W. *Number In Scripture: Its Supernatural Design and Spiritual Significance.* Grand Rapids, MI: Kregel Publications, 1967.

Davis, John J. *Biblical Numerology: A Basic Study of the Use of Numbers in the Bible.* Grand Rapids, MI: Baker Book House Company, 1968.

Strong, James. *The New Strong's Expanded Exhaustive Concordance of the Bible.* Nashville, Tennessee: Thomas Nelson Publishers, 2001.

Vine, E. W. *Expository Dictionary of the Bible.*

About the Author

Brenda Stephens is the eighth born of thirteen children born to a woman whose mother died when she was only five years old and who only completed the fifth grade in elementary school and never received another motherly guide for her life. Her mother lived a hard life, and that pasted down to all of her children with no exceptions.

Love in Brenda's life was as limited as the food on the table and the clothes on her back. But God being the gracious God that He is caused events and experiences that she could draw from so that as she learned His word, she could look back and see where love was or should have been. A few details of events are contained in the content of this book.